KU-032-707

TAKE ME HOME

Tessa Cunningham

PAN BOOKS

First published 2012 by Sidgwick & Jackson

First published in paperback 2013 by Pan Books
an imprint of Pan Macmillan, a division of Macmillan Publishers Limited
Pan Macmillan, 20 New Wharf Road, London N1 9RR
Basingstoke and Oxford
Associated companies throughout the world
www.panmacmillan.com

ISBN 978-1-4472-1129-7

Copyright © Tessa Cunningham 2012

The right of Tessa Cunningham to be identified as the
author of this work has been asserted by her in accordance
with the Copyright, Designs and Patents Act 1988.

All photographs have been provided courtesy of the author.

For reasons of privacy and to protect the identities of those
involved, some names in the book have been changed.

All rights reserved. No part of this publication may be
reproduced, stored in or introduced into a retrieval system, or
transmitted, in any form, or by any means (electronic, mechanical,
photocopying, recording or otherwise) without the prior written
permission of the publisher. Any person who does any unauthorized
act in relation to this publication may be liable to criminal
prosecution and civil claims for damages.

1 3 5 7 9 8 6 4 2

A CIP catalogue record for this book is available from
the British Library.

Printed and bound by CPI Group (UK) Ltd, Croydon, CR0 4YY

This book is sold subject to the condition that it shall not,
by way of trade or otherwise, be lent, re-sold, hired out,
or otherwise circulated without the publisher's prior consent
in any form of binding or cover other than that in which
it is published and without a similar condition including this
condition being imposed on the subsequent purchaser.

Visit www.panmacmillan.com to read more about all our books
and to buy them. You will also find features, author interviews and
news of any author events, and you can sign up for e-newsletters
so that you're always first to hear about our new releases.

3 0132 02287244 9

Tessa Cunningham was born in Farnborough. She read English at St Anne's College, Oxford, before taking a diploma in journalism at Cardiff University. Her first job in 1982 was on the *Sheffield Star*. She joined the *Sun* in 1986, working first as a news reporter, then a show-business reporter and finally as a feature writer. She has been freelance since 1991, working for a variety of publications including the *Daily Mirror*, *Bella*, *Best*, *Woman and Home* and *Woman's Own*. For the last twelve years she has worked almost exclusively for the *Daily Mail*'s Femail pages. Tessa lives in Winchester in Hampshire.

For my mother, Tess,
and sister, Hilary.

CONTENTS

Acknowledgements

I should like to thank my brothers, Andy and Simon, who racked their brains for family anecdotes and then uncomplainingly read the manuscript more times than any man should have to.

I'd like also to thank Ellen and Elise and my nieces, Frances and Sibylla, for their constant support and encouragement.

I owe a debt of gratitude to the wonderful gang of friends who have been there for me through thick and thin, showing unstinting love and kindness.

I am immensely grateful to the excellent Jonathan Conway, at Mulcahy Conway Associates, whose idea this book was, and to Ingrid and Cindy at Pan Macmillan for their unwavering enthusiasm.

Most of all, I thank Dad for loving me and believing in me.

INTRODUCTION

Walking into the stiflingly hot room, I could feel the sweat breaking out as I pinned on a smile and mentally prepared myself for the people I was about to meet. There was Minnie, who would rush over, press a Malteser into my hand and then tell me excitedly that she won't see me tomorrow as she's going home. I'd nod and tell her that I was happy for her, although I know she'd be sitting in the same green vinyl arm-chair the next day when I'd have to feign happiness for her all over again.

There was Aggie, who would want to know whether I was on duty that night. Whatever I answered, she would want to know again in five minutes. There was Geoff, who would whisper darkly that there were burglars about and urge me to keep an eye on my shoes. Truth to tell, I'd never been tempted to take my shoes off. It could have been something to do with the sticky-looking carpet tiles. But I didn't have the energy to start explaining.

There was Gladys, with the ulcerated legs so bloated that

I could hardly bear to look at them. She couldn't move very far or very fast but she would smile cheerily and call out: 'Good morning,' whatever time of day it was.

And then there was Dad. I had absolutely no idea what he made of all this. The truth was that I was too cowardly to ask because I had absolutely no idea what to do next. Just a few months before, Dad was living a perfectly normal, independent life in his own squeaky-clean flat. He cooked for himself, did his own washing, and his immaculate clothes were a testament to the fact that he was still a dab hand with the iron. He did the *Sunday Times* crossword every week, terrier-like, refusing to give up until it was complete. And his idea of bedtime reading was Shakespeare or Dickens. As I lived two streets away I popped in every few days and Dad came for lunch every Sunday, but that was the limit of my involvement in his life and his in mine.

Although he was ninety-five, the only thing troubling him was arthritis in his knees. It had forced him to give up golf and tea-dancing – a hobby he took up aged eighty-six after my mother died and which opened up a whole new life for him. But he still managed to walk to the bus stop every day – albeit with a stick – and whizz off into town where he enjoyed a cup of coffee and a cream cake in the Marks and Spencer café. His stiff upper lip and joie de vivre lulled me into the belief that things would carry on like this for ever. So it was as much a shock for me as it was for him when, in June 2010, Dad fell as he was carrying his bedtime cup of coffee the short distance from the kitchen to his armchair.

He had landed on his bottom and hadn't been able to get up again. Luckily, he had his Lifeline buzzer around his neck – something he'd taken to wearing quite recently. He'd pressed it and the call centre had rung 999 for him.

I was strolling down a street in Paris, idly wondering which restaurant to eat in that night, when my mobile phone rang and I found myself talking to Sandra, the paramedic. Dad was lying on a stretcher, about to be taken off to hospital. The line crackled as I tried to ask questions, too stunned to take in the answers. But, even in my befuddled state, her words 'I think he might have broken his hip' rang out like a clarion call.

I got her to pass the phone to Dad. Dad is incredibly deaf. Sometimes it's comical; sometimes it's infuriating. Sometimes, like at that moment, it's distressing. Motorbikes careered past me and elegant Parisians out for an evening meander stared disdainfully as I shrieked my love into the emptiness. Would he hear? Would he know? Dad was airily dismissive of the whole thing. 'Don't worry about me, love. You enjoy yourself,' he said.

But how could I? I knew that if he had broken his hip, it would mean an operation, which, at his age, could be fatal. I rang my brothers: Andy was at the Glastonbury Festival, Simon was at his flat in Edinburgh, and both sounded as shocked and helpless as I felt. Thankfully, Andy promised that he would get to Winchester the next morning.

As I put my mobile back in my handbag, I felt frightened. I also felt furious with myself – and with Dad. I'd only left home that morning. Why on earth had this happened now when I was too far away to help or to do anything about it? I'd gone to Paris for a long weekend with my daughter Ellen, who was about to turn nineteen, while Elise, her seventeen-year-old sister, was on a school trip to Nice. More importantly, Ellen was about to go to university. In September she was off to London to study History of Art at the Courtauld Institute. She was on the cusp of a new and exciting life. And this holiday was supposed to be a celebration. I'd pictured mornings spent strolling around the Louvre and the Musée d'Orsay, afternoons window shopping and evenings spent sipping glasses of chilled wine in chic cafés and talking in a way in which, back home, we never seemed to have the time to do – and might never again. What I hadn't expected was to find ourselves huddled in a restaurant that evening, talking about death.

Like most children – even grown-up women of fifty-one – I'd taken Dad's presence in my life for granted. So, of course, had Ellen. An adoring and hugely energetic grandpa, he'd taught her everything from how to skip to how to do her times tables. I tried to crystallize all the things I thought about Dad and how he'd be feeling now: 'He's had a wonderful, rich life,' I said. 'If he wants to fight on, he will. But, if he decides he's had enough, he won't be scared of dying.'

But the truth was that I was scared of him dying. So was Ellen. It wasn't just that we hadn't said goodbye. It was that we hadn't treasured him enough. He was like my toaster: I can't imagine life without it, but I don't greet it every morning with whoops of unadulterated joy and gratitude, squealing, 'Thank you for being here for me.' To be brutally honest, visiting Dad had become just one more burden in my busy life. I'd arrive in a frantic hurry, on my way to do something else, and sometimes wouldn't even bother to have a cup of tea with him. I'd check the fridge, run my fingers over the work surfaces (by now Dad had a fortnightly cleaner), and feel I'd done my duty. I told myself I'd make it up to him one day when I had more time – as though time was something I controlled. How stupid was I? Of all people, I should have known that time isn't doled out in predictable parcels and that life never stands still. It shoots off down side roads, careers into cul-de-sacs and tears up mountainsides. And then, one day, perhaps when you least expect it, it runs out all together.

Poor Ellen felt just as bad, and with much less reason. She'd been in Rome for nine months, working as an au pair. Before that she'd been studying for A levels, and before that it had been GCSEs. No wonder visiting her grandpa had got pushed slightly to the side in the whirlwind of growing up. She'd written to him from Rome, I knew, because he'd shown me her letters with such pride. But a combination of his deafness and her habit of talking at a hundred miles an hour meant that any deeper relationship had somehow foundered along the way.

'But he's always been so lovely to me,' she sobbed. 'Does he know how much I love him?'

I knew he did. I hoped he knew how much I loved him

too. But that didn't make either of us feel that much better. As for Elise, I didn't dare tell her the news. She unequivocally adored her grandpa and I decided that there was no point distressing her when there was nothing she, or any of us, could do.

Andy was on the phone the next morning. He was in Winchester and Dad was about to have an operation to replace his shattered hip. Andy seemed calm. I tried to be so too. But the relief was indescribable when – some six hours later – Andy rang to say that the operation had gone well. Dad had not needed a general anaesthetic. He had come out the other end.

But, although I knew things would never be quite the same again, I didn't realize just how fragile Dad now was until I got home two days later. Propped up in his hospital bed, he looked shrunken and almost childishly lost. As he hugged me, he struggled to recount what had happened to him and seemed confused as to why he was in pain. 'They tell me I've had an operation,' he kept repeating. 'I don't remember anything.'

'Never mind, Dad. You'll soon be back on your feet,' I blustered. And part of me hoped it was true. Dad had always been so active and vigorous, it was impossible to imagine him not pelting around the place as normal.

But, although Dad's robust health meant he rallied remarkably well after the operation, the toll was still huge. A combination of his arthritis and the invasive surgery meant that he was pathetically doddery. After two weeks, he started physiotherapy. He was encouraged out of bed and issued with a Zimmer frame.

It seemed both ludicrous and tragic. Dad had always pooh-poohed the idea of needing a walking frame. 'They're for poor old cripples,' he had harrumphed. Now here he was, meekly accepting his fate – only he didn't quite. Despite tucking into his hospital dinners with gusto – the only person on earth who could eagerly lap up foul-smelling fish pie and jam roly-poly and custard every day of the week – he talked wistfully of getting home. 'Once I get rid of this thing,' he'd say, gesturing impatiently at his Zimmer frame, 'I'll be getting out and about again. I might even be able to go dancing now I have a new hip!'

I wanted to believe him. Trusting your parent knows best is a hard habit to break. The doctors were reluctant to give a prognosis. 'Anything could happen,' they said. So, three weeks after his accident, I packed Dad's bag, helped him into a hospital wheelchair, and drove him the short distance to a local authority care home, which was happy to provide a temporary room and carers while he gained the strength to live independently again in his own flat.

Looking around his little bedroom with its en suite bathroom and kitchen, I tried to ignore the smell of old clothes and microwaved stews. Mercifully, Dad has always had the knack of making the best of things and letting awkward situations wash over him.

'This is great.' He grinned, examining the reading light beside his bed. 'I've got every home comfort.'

I felt a twinge of embarrassment as I rather too readily agreed.

I told myself that it was only a temporary solution until Dad got back on his feet. But as the days merged into weeks, it became clear that Dad wasn't getting any better. He was too physically frail to walk up stairs. He couldn't stand without his frame – and even then he could only manage to hobble across a room before collapsing in pain into the nearest chair. Not being able to stand meant that he couldn't manage to do the simplest tasks for himself any more. He couldn't dress himself and, worst of all, he couldn't wash himself. Carers had to do even the most intimate things for him.

I didn't know whether to be sad or relieved, but Dad didn't rail against the situation. In fact, he took it all in his stride, claiming to revel in the attention. 'The carers even wash my feet. I feel like an Arab potentate, surrounded by waiting women,' he joked.

He seemed oblivious to the rather challenging behaviour of his elderly fellow residents. Unlike Dad, who was there purely for rehabilitation, most of them lived in the home permanently because they could no longer cope mentally or physically by themselves. Mainly women – a corollary of the fact that women outlive men – they congregated in the sitting room from breakfast until tea. Needless to say, as the new arrival – and a dapper-looking man to boot – Dad was fussed over constantly. They vied over whom he'd sit with, stroked his hair, kissed him goodnight and told me repeatedly what a good boy he was.

At first, when they weren't looking, Dad would grimace and pretend to wring their necks – impatient at all their fussing. 'They're very effusive,' he'd hiss. But, as time passed, he became increasingly accepting of the whole situation. He no longer read his books and, when I came to visit, he no longer asked when he'd be going home. It was almost as though he was accepting his fate and giving up on life – or, at least, on all the things he'd once enjoyed in life.

'It's not too bad here, love,' he told me one day. 'I could get used to it.'

The truth was that I was coming to accept that he'd never be going home again. And – although Dad has always been given to wildly unrealistic ideas – so was he. Even with carers, his life would be joyless. Dad's two-bedroom flat was up a steep flight of stairs and had yet more stairs outside the building. Once he was inside, getting out again would be an almost impossible undertaking for him.

A care home – if not this one, then another one – seemed the only solution. Reluctantly, my brothers and I started talking about local options. But then one day something happened – something so imperceptible I almost missed it.

I took Dad's hand to say goodbye and, as he kissed my cheek, his hand – how did it get to be so small and frail without me noticing? – held on to mine just a little too long. And as I looked into his eyes, I saw all the yearning he was far too proud and far too loving to articulate: *'I'm scared. Please take me home.'*

I've always hated goodbyes. There have been too many in my life. Some achingly long-drawn-out, some dramatic, some bitter, and some so sudden that I didn't even get a chance to say the words. But this one was so gentle and so dignified, it took my breath away. And I hadn't even seen it coming.

I thought of all the reasons why Dad couldn't live with me. I had a demanding, time-consuming job as a journalist; my house was up for sale; I'd just recovered from breast cancer; I was in the throes of getting divorced; Ellen was about to go to university and Elise would be following in a matter of months. What more upheaval did I possibly need? I craved my old life back, before all the stress and trauma turned it upside down. But somehow – compelling though they were – none of the reasons seemed good enough when faced with the blindingly obvious. Living with me, Dad would be happy. And, surely, I wouldn't be too unhappy, would I?

And so, that day in August 2010, I jumped in and offered him a home with me. It was to be many months and after a close proximity with Dad before I realized that I was simply doing what I'd learnt from him – following my gut instinct and charging in regardless of the consequences. Dad would come and live with me for as long as it worked. My brothers were relieved. The girls were excited. Many of my friends – particularly those with ageing parents – thought I was mad and worried it would be far too much for me. As for

Dad, joy lit up his face but he still tried to talk me out of it.

'I won't be much help to you, darling,' he admitted rue-fully.

It was the understatement of the century, I thought, as I started coming to my senses and realizing what a huge amount of preparation was involved and how many hurdles were strewn in the way. My list went something like this: a) tell ex-husband I am no longer selling the house; b) come up with a new plan to raise money to provide his share of the equity; c) ring Derek the plumber to arrange building a bathroom for Dad; d) sort out the entire contents of Dad's flat so that it could be rented out; and e) cancel social life for foreseeable future.

But how wrong I was. Ever since he moved in with his Zimmer frame, his collection of hearing-aid batteries and monogrammed hankies and his tins of Black Bullets boiled sweets, Dad has been helping me more than I could ever have imagined. And he's done it just by being Dad.

The brutal truth is that, when Dad moved in, my life was in freefall. Consumed by anger and fear, I was reeling from the aftershocks of all that had happened and I was fright-ened by all I still had to face. Now I was thundering down the track and smack into two more hurdles: I had to sell my house and I had to face waving goodbye to Ellen when she moved out. I'd learnt enough from what had happened to be sure that nothing lasts for ever – not good health, not marriages (or, at least, not mine) – and that's why I was probably much more sanguine about giving Dad a home than I would have been even a few years earlier. It was a good plan for now and that was good enough.

But I didn't anticipate that living with Dad would provide me with a crash course in self-healing. Dad is the least guru-like figure you could possibly imagine. He can't abide moaners, is given to wildly tactless remarks and, as he's deaf, definitely isn't the best listener in the world. But he's taught himself how to cope with enough trauma and tragedy to fell most people. Looking back down the long tunnel of history of a life begun in 1915 – in the midst of the First World War – there's very little he hasn't seen or experienced.

Every day I've been amazed by something new that pops out of his mouth – wise, witty or just plain common sense – a testament to a life well lived and a heart still beating powerfully. But it's not just what he says, it's what he does – it's the very tenets by which he lives his life. When I last shared a home with Dad, it was 1977 and I was nineteen, heading off to Oxford University and desperate for independence. I didn't give two hoots for what Dad thought about anything. While I loved and respected him, I certainly didn't think I needed him or had anything left to learn from him.

But – in the most subtle and delightful way imaginable – living with Dad has proved to be an education. He's taught me how to let go of the past and he's shown me how to relish every second of the present. I've learnt how to forgive myself for the things I did wrong and to give myself credit for the things I did right. Of course, some of the lessons I'd already learnt as a little girl at my dad's knee; I just didn't always know how to put them into practice.

So here, courtesy of my dad, I offer you an education in happiness. I hope you don't need his lessons as much as I did.

ONE

YOU'LL ALWAYS BE
MY LITTLE GIRL

I've often wondered what would have happened if I'd left Dad sitting stoically in the care home on that fateful day, gone home, canvassed the opinions of friends and family, and then thought long and hard about all that I would need to do, and all that I would be giving up before he could move in.

Would I have thought the better of it? Would I have decided it was all going to be too stressful, too much of a responsibility? Quite possibly. But I didn't and I hadn't. I guess the truth is that life had been so spectacularly un-predictable over the last few years that I wasn't scared of change in the way I once had been. I'd never planned for this moment. Dad had always been so fit and strong. I'd rather imagined that he would simply drop down dead on the golf course or the dance floor one day. The thought of my ener-getic, irrepressible dad being infirm and confined to a nursing home had always seemed inconceivable – and it still did. So, while I hadn't actively planned for Dad to move in with me,

I'd not ruled it out as a possibility either. I just hadn't planned for the moment I would actually have to make a decision. But, here it was, and my heart was yelling: 'Do it! Do it!' And I knew, however daunting it might prove, I was doing the right thing.

'The girls will love having you live with us. So will I,' I promised.

'It will be wonderful to be part of a family again, seeing all the comings and goings and the general kerfuffle,' he said. 'But you do know, sweet, that I'm an old man and I won't be able to help much.'

'Of course, Daddy. Don't worry. I can do it all. I'll start making arrangements now,' I said. And, as I kissed him goodbye, I promised myself that I would make it work.

Even so, the enormity of what I was letting myself in for hit me like a bolt between the eyes as soon as I got home. As Dad couldn't manage stairs, he was going to have to live on the ground floor. My sitting room could be his bed-sitting room. It's a lovely light, airy room with two huge bay windows overlooking the road, but so big and so formal that we barely ever used it, preferring to hunker down in the basement instead where the kitchen and family room are. But Dad would need a separate bathroom on the same floor and it rapidly became obvious that there was only one solution: our garden room would have to be Dad's bathroom.

As I looked around the room and contemplated all the work involved, I was filled with the most peculiar mixture of fear and excitement. The garden room was the last project

Richard and I had worked on before our marriage ended. It was Richard's favourite room. Every nook and cranny reminded me of him and of a time when I'd imagined our life together going on for ever. We'd chosen the yellow and cream paint scheme together and agonized together over whether we could afford the marble floor. Richard had designed the floor-to-ceiling glass doors to make the garden appear to reach into the room, while the little iron coffee table, the dusky-pink sofa from his bachelor days and the drinks trolley, inherited from his dad's cousin, were all arranged to offer the promise of total relaxation. On the floor, huge pots of hydrangeas and rhododendrons, which always reminded me of my green-fingered mother, soaked up the sun dappling through the Victorian-style etched-glass windows. On balmy summer nights, we had sat on the sofa, sipping wine and sharing a bowl of olives while listening to music. I'd lain on the sofa and read my way through the after-effects of chemo treatment. Huge, meaty books I'd never have started otherwise: *War and Peace*, *Anna Karenina*, *Middlemarch*, *Barchester Towers*, *Wives and Daughters*. In short, all the books I'd promised myself I'd read one day – never guessing that day would arrive with a cancer diagnosis.

It was in this room that guests had mingled on my forty-ninth birthday party, the one I'd held not to be contrary but simply because I didn't know whether I'd reach fifty. I was halfway through my chemotherapy treatment, exhausted and weepy. I remembered Richard weaving around the room with champagne bottles, glancing over his shoulder every so often to smile at me and check that I was OK – not too tired, not too sick. And it was in this room, a year later, that my marriage ended.

Now here I was about to dismantle it, consigning to history the life Richard and I had built together, and I was filled with the most peculiar mixture of emotions. A huge part of me felt: 'Hooray. At last.' I was elated at the prospect of breathing new life into my home, and this room in particular, which had seemed so bleak and empty since Richard left. Buoyed up on a tidal wave of adrenaline, I'd rushed around the house like a whirling dervish in the weeks after he moved out, stripping the house of all the pictures, ornaments and photos that reminded me of him. I'd hidden everything in the attic so that I wouldn't have to see it again and then I'd collapsed. But since then I'd been living in limbo, allowing the house to atrophy around me because I was too wary of the emotions I might unleash by having to think too hard about any of the possessions that were once ours and were now only mine. Suddenly, with Dad coming, I had a burning reason to make changes. As I thought of Dad's eagerness and excitement at moving in, I felt the thrill of a new chapter opening. The problem was how to negotiate all the practical things that I needed to do to get there.

The first thing I did was ring Derek, the plumber. He'd known Dad for almost twenty years and had become the family handyman along the way. As soon as I explained my predicament he promised he'd get on the case. He called in the next day and, to my relief, agreed that while creating the bathroom wouldn't be easy, it was definitely possible.

'You know what Dad's like. He's champing at the bit to get here. So how soon can you do it?' I asked.

Derek smiled ruefully. 'I know he'd like me to start tomorrow and have it done by the end of the day, but it'll have to be next week. Any chance of keeping Mr Cunningham quiet until then?'

I wasn't banking on it. I knew Dad would be virtually counting the minutes until he could move in. To say that Dad is impatient is like describing the North Pole as being a little chilly, or vindaloo curries as being a tad on the spicy side. Dad has no conception of how to bide his time. Trying to stop him from doing something the second the idea pops into his head is like trying to restrain a pack of slavering gun dogs in hot pursuit of a fox. And as for Dad letting grass grow under his feet – it's as likely to sprout up in the Sahara Desert as it is to grow under his size eight brogues. Getting Dad to stand in a queue, sit in traffic, or even wait for a TV programme to start without flicking impatiently through the channels has always been well nigh impossible. He's been the same ever since I can remember. And if family folklore is anything to go by, he always has been. Then again, it's hard to find too much fault with his impatience – after all, it's how he came to marry my mother.

My mother's best friend, Pat, was Dad's cousin. Her mother was Dad's father's sister. During the Second World

War, Dad, a flight lieutenant with the RAF, was stationed briefly outside Birmingham, only a few miles from Pat's home, and he promised his parents that as soon as he had leave he'd visit for the weekend.

So one summer's day in 1943, Dad rocked up in his smart officer's uniform, looking like Laurence Olivier as Heathcliff – all dark hair, brooding eyes and thick Geordie accent. His cousins and aunt sat him down and clucked over him. Then they poured him tea, offered him rock cakes and prepared for a pleasant afternoon catching up on family gossip. Dad, however, had other ideas. He'd barely gulped down his tea and bolted down his bun before he was shooting out of his chair and pacing around the room, fiddling with their ornaments and asking eagerly if any odd jobs needed doing.

They couldn't think of anything to keep him occupied, so Pat decided to call for reinforcements. She rang my mother, who lived in the next street and was known for being good fun and quick-witted enough to handle most situations.

'Tess, come quick,' she said. 'We've got our cousin Jimmy with us and we don't know what to do with him. He won't sit still. We've run out of conversation and we're at our wits' end.'

My mother found herself marching up and down the garden beside Dad, mesmerised by this tornado of energy, so different from the buttoned-up, stuffy boyfriends she was used to from the tennis club.

They might never have met again. But, perhaps inspired

by Dad's stories – he was a veteran of the Battle of Britain –
Mum, who was training to be a nurse to help in the war
effort and was loathing every minute of it, decided to ask
for a transfer to the WAAF. She was picked to train as a me-
teorologist, tracking weather conditions, and was posted to
London for a month's induction. Dad also happened to be in
London. Mum always claimed that Pat innocently suggested
that, as they were both in London, Dad should take her out.
But I suspect Mum put her up to it. Mum being Mum, she
just never wanted to admit to anything even slightly under-
hand.

So my parents found themselves enjoying tea and cake
in the Lyons tea house near Buckingham Palace Road where
Mum was billeted, while the bombs dropped all around
them. And, after just four meetings, Dad – in typical Dad
fashion – asked Mum to marry him.

My mother had made the mistake of explaining to Dad
that she was unofficially engaged – and had been since the
outbreak of war.

'But that's preposterous. What's he thinking of? I'd marry
you instantly if I could,' Dad said. And, as Mum was soon to
be posted to the Far East, which would mean that they might
not see each other again for many years, he suggested they
do just that. Get married instantly – or at least within the
week. How could Mum resist?

Her parents were horrified. Her father, the treasurer
of what was then the borough of Sutton Coldfield in Birmingham, had imagined a suitor who was somewhat more

genteel and middle-class than my Dad, who came from an impoverished background in Newcastle. The other stumbling block, in his mind, was that Dad was about to be posted to Normandy in the wake of the D-Day landings for what was to prove the final push to Berlin.

'I really don't want my daughter to be a widow,' Grandpa Connon said crisply.

'I don't go much on the idea either, sir. And believe me, I'll do my best to stay alive,' Dad retorted smartly.

My parents married on 23 August 1944; Dad in uniform, Mum in a suit she had sewn herself. They honeymooned in Stratford-upon-Avon – courtesy of the local police force. Dad had asked his sergeant to book him a room. The sergeant was duly waiting at the station in Stratford, only to inform the happy new bridegroom that he'd had no luck. The town had been overrun with evacuees from the bombing of Birmingham and there was no room at the inn. Never one to be beaten, Dad marched straight off to the local nick.

'I'm here on my honeymoon, officer. Any chance you can help me out?' he asked with his usual Geordie charm. Half an hour later, Mum and Dad were ensconced in the finest hotel room in Stratford-on-Avon. And, three days later, Dad was in France.

It didn't take long for Mum to realize that Dad's impetuosity comes as naturally to him as breathing. The war was over. My sister Hilary had arrived. It was the second day in their new home in Sutton Coldfield and Mum was talking dreamily about the improvements she'd like to make over time.

'Jimmy, what do you think about having a hatch from the kitchen to the dining room – then I'd be able to pass food through and you could put it on the table? It would make everything so much easier,' she said.

Dad's eyes lit up with eager enthusiasm. Immediately, he was on his feet. Before Mum could stop him, he had found his hammer and chisel and was bashing away at the wall, scattering gritty cement dust all over the breakfast table.

'What do you reckon, love? I just need to get it plastered and it's all done,' he announced, a grin of boyish satisfaction on his face, before grabbing his coat to rush off to the hardware shop.

Barely half an hour later, my anxious mother was watching Dad slap plaster on the gaping hole with his bare fingers.

'Don't you need a trowel for that?' she asked quizzically, remembering her father, who would never have started even the smallest task without meticulous planning.

'Oh, no need to bother,' said Dad, who was in far too much of a hurry and having far too much fun to go hunting for more equipment. And, to be fair, the serving hatch may have looked rough and ready but it was in operation by lunchtime.

Mum never managed to change him. Actually, I'm not sure that she really wanted to. Dad's impetuosity has always been part of his immense charm. But it can also be intensely irritating. There wasn't a single wall in our house which didn't have a huge thumbprint on it because Dad couldn't wait long enough to check whether the paint was dry. Pictures hung wonkily because Dad seemed to think that using a spirit level was cheating. It was the same with manufacturers' instruction manuals – when he got his first video recorder, Dad had barely ushered the delivery driver out of the door before he set to work. He had the recorder set up in twenty minutes and sat back down jubilantly. He only realized that there might be a slight problem when he attempted to record *Antiques Roadshow* and ended up with a blank screen and no sound. He had no clue as to how to eject the video, and Mum found him trying to prise it out of the machine with a butter knife. Sheepishly, he had to agree with Mum's suggestion of calling out an engineer to do the job properly. He promised faithfully that, in future, he would look at the instruction manual first. As if.

Now Dad's eagerness knew no bounds. According to him he could move in within the week, even kipping down on the floor in a sleeping bag if necessary, while the bathroom was being built. And it wasn't just the bathroom. I also had to clear out his apartment so that I could rent it. That way I'd have enough money to pay for his care. Fortunately, as Dad's needs had been assessed when he left hospital, we already had a care package set up and ready to go. A carer would come in the morning to help him get washed and dressed, at lunchtime to make him a bowl of soup – freeing me up to work – and again in the evening to help him get ready for bed. All I had to do was find the money – some

£600 a month. My brothers agreed that renting out Dad's apartment was the best option. But first I had to get the apartment decorated – another job for Derek.

Sorting out both my home and Dad's apartment was so all-consuming that it didn't give me any time to think about the other huge change on the horizon. I had almost forgotten that, as Dad moved in, Ellen would be moving out. And, in another twelve months, Elise might well be going to university too. Ellen was going to start her three-year degree course in History of Art and, as the date loomed, her excitement was mounting. She had a room in a hall of residence on the Strand. I longed to share her joy but I was too scared. Not for her, but for me and how I would cope without her. I'd miss her. I'd miss my job as her mum. I'd guided her through every one of her school days. I'd helped her read, listened patiently as she stumblingly repeated over her times tables, and less patiently as she practised the violin hour after screeching hour. I'd been there when she took her first step and lost her first tooth. My first baby: I knew the second she was put in my arms and a shaft of late-August sun illuminated her scrunched-up little face that I had found the love of my life. After that it often seemed that we were learning together – a newborn baby with a novice mum.

Taking her out during those first months, pride and joy jostled with terror. One day when I was wheeling her along in her little blue pram, we ran into a team of workmen digging up the road. I was so petrified that the noise of the drilling had damaged her eardrums that I raced her to the doctor, who, mercifully, managed to keep a straight face. Then there was the time when she wandered off at the park to look at the ducks. Finally I found her, chatting to another family. As I hugged her far too tight, I realized that she held my happiness in her hands. Just thinking about it all these years later, my stomach still turns to jelly.

Watching time racing by, I was determined not to forget a thing. I bought a little book and wrote down all the funny, quirky things Ellen said, like when, aged four, she met me at the school gates and announced that she'd just had a 'gym and tonic' lesson. Luckily, the teacher was out of earshot and remained oblivious to my evening tipple. Or how she looked at my feet before announcing sagely: 'Mummy, I love you. But you have ugly feet like a troll.'

Now, at nineteen, and with the university place she had worked so hard for in the bag, she was striding off into a fantastic new life. I felt an enormous sense of relief and satisfaction in a job well done. But I also felt an aching sense of loss. Overnight I would be redundant.

I couldn't bear to think of all I'd miss without her: Ellen's gentle way of bringing me back to earth when I get stressed. The evenings gossiping over the kitchen table. The clothes shopping trips when somehow she always says the right thing while still guiding me away from anything that makes my bum look big. I'd tried to shield her from the terror I felt as I coped with cancer, but I couldn't hide the love I felt for her and Elise, nor my fear of leaving them. For the last eight years, at least, I'd been moaning non-stop about the state of her bedroom. But now I couldn't bear to imagine the day when it would be stripped bare: posters peeled off the walls; wardrobe emptied; the tangle of tights, knickers, loose change and empty water bottles swept up off the floor, the mouldy coffee cups vanished for ever.

So, instead I threw all my energy into sorting out Dad's move, grateful for a distraction. Problems that might have appeared insurmountable a few months earlier were now a welcome diversion. Apart from the logistics of organizing his apartment, the biggest stumbling block was the whacking great For Sale sign outside my own house. After much fraught negotiation with lawyers, I'd agreed to put the house on the market eighteen months after Richard left, and to split the equity – 80 per cent to me and 20 per cent to him. The house had finally gone up for sale in May and I'd geared myself up to moving somewhere smaller. But now, with Dad's fall, everything had changed and I thanked my lucky stars that no one had shown a flicker of interest. It meant that I could stay in the house and buy Richard out – if I could find the money.

Talking it over with my brothers and my grown-up nieces Frances and Sibylla, my sister Hilary's children, we came up with a plan. Simon had recently retired from his job as an economist with the United Nations and now lived in Edinburgh. He had just sold his property in New York and he offered to invest his spare cash in my house. It was a massive weight off my shoulders and I was hugely touched. I knew, unlike Andy, who lives relatively close by in Brighton, that Simon wouldn't be able to visit Dad regularly or do much to help out practically. This was his way of contributing and it made me feel much less alone with the responsibility. Meanwhile, Frances and Sibylla both promised that they'd visit regularly and would help out if ever I needed them to. Even so, as Dad's arrival date – 29 September – edged closer, I began to worry whether I wasn't blinding myself to the massive job I was taking on and the huge sea change in my life.

What if Dad and I simply didn't get on? What if we couldn't handle the roles we now found ourselves in – he the needy old man; me the bossy mother? We hadn't shared a house for over thirty years. And when we did, it was his home and I was a child. Now the tables were dramatically turned in a way neither of us would ever have chosen. He was coming to live in my home because he needed my help. And I feared I wasn't compassionate enough or – even at fifty-one – mature enough to handle the change.

I railed against what time had done to him. Every time I visited Dad in the home, he seemed older and more shrunken. One day his jersey was spattered with soup and my usually meticulous dad hadn't even noticed. Where once he had joked with me about the over-eager attentions of the elderly ladies who fussed over him, now he submitted without protest. In fact, he barely seemed to notice. And having any sort of conversation with him was proving increasingly difficult. Despite his deafness, he used to make an effort to listen. Now the effort seemed too much and I got tired of having to repeat the same boring platitudes time after time: 'What did you have for lunch today?' 'What have you been watching on TV?' I wanted the dad I remembered: big, strong and dependable. And I was terribly worried that Dad was now too far down the road for me to cope.

I hankered after the life that was disappearing. I wanted to be the focal point in my daughters' lives as I had been when they were little. I wanted my dad on the periphery, contentedly doing his own thing in the background. But the opposite was happening.

The day came when I had to drive Ellen to university. It was just four days before Dad was due to arrive. Aware that I was dreading the moment, my friend Helen offered to help. Tearing along the M3 and weaving our way around the Kings Road to the Strand, we made the oddest convoy: Helen and Elise leading the party in Helen's blue Mini piled high with bedding and pots and pans; Ellen and I following behind with clothes, books, make-up and anything else we could squeeze into the boot of my Golf.

As we helped Ellen unpack and watched her nervously make small talk with the girls in her corridor, who we desperately hoped would become her friends, it was hard not to think back thirty-three years to October 1977 when Helen and I met: two naïve, swotty girls staring at each other over a plate of broccoli – a vegetable so exotic that we didn't even know its name – in the dining hall of St Anne's College, Oxford on our first day as English undergraduates. That day – and, in truth, all the weeks and months that followed – I

was so engrossed in my new life, so overjoyed to be independent, that I hadn't given a fig for how my mum and dad
must have felt as they had driven away, their car as empty as
my heart now felt.

Ellen grabbed me in a huge bear hug. 'I'm going to miss
you so much, Mum,' she said.

'Oh, I'll be fine. I've got lots to do with Grandpa moving
in,' I said, hoping she wouldn't notice the wobble in my
voice as I steeled myself to leave and not look back.

In fact, there was so much to do over the next few
days that I barely had time to notice that Ellen was gone, let
alone miss her. I began to feel my head was going to burst
thinking about all the jobs: sorting through Dad's possessions – deciding which to bring to his new home, which to
give away; fitting a key safe beside the front door so that the
carers could come and go; buying a new cooker for Dad's
old flat; letting his lunch club know his new address; buying
bed linen and towels. The list seemed to grow every day.
Cocooned in the care home, Dad wasn't able to do a thing.

'I'm sorry that I'm not able to be much use to you,' he
said regretfully.

I tried not to mind but I was beginning to feel a twinge
of resentment. I was frightened about what it was actually
going to feel like, effectively being on call twenty-four hours
a day. I still knew that I was doing the right thing. After all,
Dad's my dad and I owe him. But I was much less sure that
I was actually going to be able to do it any other way than
through gritted teeth.

And then the moment came. I wheeled Dad in through the garden room – now magically transformed into a bath-room – and into his bed-sitting room. He looked around, taking in all the furniture from his old home, his favourite painting of Frans Hals's *The Laughing Cavalier* on the wall, photos of Mum on the mantelpiece, and he was so stunned that it was a good few minutes before he could speak.

'It's wonderful, my treasure, simply wonderful,' he said, his eyes misting up. And then, as the family dog Milo came bounding in to greet him, all puppyish enthusiasm, Dad broke into a huge grin. He has always loved dogs and I hoped that, if I were too busy to spend much time with Dad, at least Milo could be a companion for him.

I felt a huge surge of satisfaction. Dad was here. He was happy. I'd done it. As I helped him into his armchair in front of the TV and offered him a cup of tea, I began to hope that this new life wouldn't be too bad after all. I could cope. It might even be nice to have someone need me again, even if it weren't the one person I wanted to be needing me: Ellen. I deliberately hadn't rung her because I didn't want to make her homesick. And she hadn't rung me either. I hoped it was because she was having too much fun in Freshers' Week. But anxiety and loss nagged at me.

With Dad settled, I took the opportunity to take Milo for a walk. Having to check Dad would be OK, explaining patiently where I was going and how long I'd be away for, felt strange. But the walk cleared my head. However, as I ambled home, I looked at my watch and realized that I'd been gone much longer than I'd said. I felt a pang of guilt. I'd simply have to get used to having someone rely on me again.

As I reached home, I saw Dad's face at the window, peering out anxiously. My pulse was racing as I dashed up to the front door. Was he all right? Did he need me? Had something dreadful happened?

'What is it, Dad?' I asked as I stumbled through the door, flooded with guilt and fear.

Dad looked perplexed. 'Nothing's the matter. I was just worried because you'd been gone so long. I know it's silly, sweet, and you've got to forgive me, but you know you'll always be my little girl and I can't stop worrying about you.'

My heart lurched. And suddenly I saw not the frail old man who could barely stand but my father – strong, dependable and always there for me. And I realized in that moment that however much my dad now needed me, he would still lay down his life for me. In his eyes I was eternally young and nothing could ever shake his love or his willingness to shield me from pain. Our roles had shifted, but he would never stop being my daddy.

And I knew with a sudden burst of joy that, however far from home my girls went, I would always be a vital part of their lives and they of mine. They would always want to be my 'little girls', as I wanted to be Dad's.

It hit home in the most unexpected way that night. After days of silence, Ellen rang. She was eager to tell me all that had been happening. I was thrilled to hear from her at last and genuinely delighted to hear her bubbling with excitement. She wanted to know all about how Grandpa had settled in. Was he happy? Was I sure I wasn't getting too stressed?

'I didn't want to ring before because I thought I might get upset. I miss you,' she said. 'Promise you'll ring every day, otherwise I'll worry about you.'

'Worry about me? Isn't that what I'm supposed to say to you?' I laughed.

As I assured her I was absolutely fine, that Grandpa was a joy and that I was thrilled she was happy, I realized it was all true. And even if it weren't, I'd fight like a tiger to stop her having to worry about me. That's what parents always do. But feeling mothered by my little girl just for that instant felt intensely sweet. I sensed then that the deep core of my love for my daughters and for Dad will never change. To me they will always be young, beautiful and unbearably precious – my 'little girls'. But you can show love in many different ways.

For the moment, Ellen didn't need my daily care. Dad did. And that was my job – for now.

TWO

YOU'RE NEVER TOO OLD
TO LEARN NEW TRICKS

It's 6 a.m. and I'm jolted awake by the sound of blaring music and disembodied voices. In the early morning confusion it takes me a while to realize that there's not an impromptu teenage party going on outside my bedroom door. It's Dad and his hellishly inconvenient dawn rendezvous with Radio 4's *Today* programme. Still, it's a marginal improvement on yesterday and the shipping forecast blaring from Dad's crackly old Roberts radio at 5 a.m. I think of my poor neighbours. I think of poor me. And I wonder if I can get a few more moments of sleep before Milo joins in the cacophony, thrilled that the household appears to be in full swing already.

Starting the day an hour earlier than I'm used to is just one of the unexpected adjustments I'm having to make. Dad, as I'm discovering, is eager to greet the day at the earliest possible opportunity. And no wonder. His days are precious – he's acutely aware that every day of good health is a bonus. They are also action-packed with a giddy round of social opportunities and Dad, old charmer that he is, grasps each chance to chat with relish.

First through the door at 8 a.m. is Laura, his morning carer. 'My pyjama girl,' Dad calls her fondly because she helps him out of bed and out of his pyjamas then gets him spruced up, washed, shaved and dressed. Laura always calls him James and teases him when he's reluctant to be dragged out of his warm bed.

'Come on, let's be having you, James, or it will be the ice-cold flannel for you,' she threatens.

'Ooh, you're such a bully,' he chides her as he snuggles under the duvet.

Later, I hear him call from the bathroom: 'Sack her. She's useless.' I look in to see her tenderly bathing his eyes with warm cotton-wool buds and Dad in seventh heaven.

'So you don't love me any more?' Laura asks, wiping away mock tears.

'Oh well, I'll forgive you because you're so pretty,' Dad says as she bends down to ruffle the hair she's just carefully washed.

Laura's thirty-four, passionate about horses and lives with her boyfriend and two dogs. She treats Dad with the same brusque no-nonsense affection you'd bestow on a beloved elderly dog. 'Sparring is the best medicine. It keeps him on his toes,' she says firmly.

Without his hearing aids, Dad is totally deaf. But with a mixture of pantomime acting and bellowing in his 'good' – as in not completely stone-deaf – ear, Laura manages to have long and animated conversations with him. One morning, I walk past the bathroom door to hear them both singing: 'I'm forever blowing bubbles . . . '

I've never heard Dad sing this particular song before. 'Where on earth did that come from?' I ask Laura, who's in a particularly giggly mood.

'I started singing for a laugh. But I only know the first line. James took over. Would you believe it? He knows the whole thing.'

Rebecca alternates with Laura as Dad's night-time carer. With a bob that might be blond one week, red the next and fingernails that, despite her job, are always perfectly painted and beautifully manicured, she looks sixteen, is actually nearer thirty and has two little boys to run around after.

Alison covers lunchtimes. She is preternaturally cheerful, totally unflappable but always in a tearing hurry. If I'm in the house at the time, I've learnt to grit my teeth when she prepares Dad's soup. It's only a simple job of heating up half a carton in the microwave, but the soup always bubbles and splatters everywhere. Dad adores her. I think he recognizes a kindred spirit in the catering department.

As well as the carers, there's Helena, who arrives every Tuesday to give Dad Holy Communion. As a cradle Catholic, he prays every night before he goes to sleep and deeply regrets the fact that he can no longer get to church every Sunday.

Then there's Robert, a volunteer who pops around once a fortnight for a cup of tea and a chat with Dad. Dad's normally more comfortable with women than he is with men, but he's taken to Robert. Perhaps it's down to their shared background in the RAF, albeit forty years apart. He also likes the fact that Robert conspires with him to wangle extra biscuits from me.

'Robert adores custard creams so much,' wheedles sweet-toothed Dad when Robert is due. 'Put a few more out, will you, love.'

Dad's old dancing partners are regular visitors. So are his former neighbours. There's Val, who cuts his hair and insists on giving Dad a cuddle before she leaves because he reminds her of her own late father whom she clearly adored. There's Wendi, the chiropodist who tells him every time she visits that he's the handsomest fellow in Winchester. The parish priest, Father John, pops around, although he's careful now to give some warning after the time he arrived unannounced. Dad was cloistered in the bathroom when I tapped gingerly on the door to report his visitor's unexpected arrival. 'Oh hell and damnation!' Dad bellowed, so deaf he's convinced that everyone except him is permanently whispering.

Valerie is also a frequent visitor. She used to clean Dad's apartment and quickly became a trusted friend, to Dad and now to me, too.

We got to know Valerie after she put a card through Dad's letterbox. She already had one client in his building and had a few spare hours to offer anyone who wanted a cleaner. Up until then, Dad had cheerfully handed over his £2 coins to the girls, who took it in turns to go and clean his flat on Saturday mornings. They quickly learnt that Dad was satisfied if they sprayed Mr Pledge liberally on his Ercol dining table, moved a few photo frames arbitrarily, and then settled down with him for a cup of coffee and a Kit Kat. It pleased Dad, but it didn't stop the flat looking increasingly grimy. Dad was finding it harder to get into corners with the vacuum cleaner and his failing eyesight meant huge swathes of the flat were missed altogether. So I asked Valerie to come for a couple of hours once a fortnight. It was one of the best decisions I ever made.

Long before she started cleaning for a living, Valerie was a live-in carer. She's super intelligent, incredibly practical and immensely kind. She's become a family friend. In the early days it was very comforting to know that I had someone to call on if I ever needed advice or practical help. She's like my own personal Super Nurse – full of tips and hints on how to make living with an elderly chap easier.

She's the one person with whom I can happily spend an entire morning debating the merits of various brands of cod liver oil and the possible side-effects of too many prunes without feeling even remotely embarrassed. And as time goes on and Dad can't easily be left for more than a few hours, Valerie offers to come and sit with him whenever I need her. 'It will be a pleasure,' she says in a way that makes me almost believe her. 'I'm so fond of your dad and we can have a nice chat.'

Dad still knows how to charm people. When Valerie arrives, he beams happily. 'I might get the occasional cup of tea,' he hints broadly.

Valerie got rid of her TV some years ago after deciding there was nothing she wanted to watch. Now she makes good use of her spare time by knitting. She always has some-thing on the go – a jumper, hat or scarves. Dad loves to watch her knit. It reminds him of Mum.

Then there are all the outings. They may not be the sort of jollies I'd choose for myself, but then I'm not Dad. Whenever he's bored, he'll dream up some problem with his hearing aids so that he can visit the local drop-in centre at the hospital's ear, nose and throat clinic. Open three times a week, it's run by volunteers on a first-come-first-served basis. You take a number, just like at a deli counter, and wait and wait and wait. At first I didn't realize why my normally impatient dad was happy to while away an hour or so with-out complaint. While I flicked through dog-eared copies of magazines which unfailingly fell open on the page offering Stannah Stairlifts and wide-fitting shoes, Dad chatted cheer-fully to the other patients who are mostly elderly. Like him, most of them, I suspect, treat the event as a bit of a social get-together. Some greeted him by name and the volunteers all knew him.

It isn't all plain sailing, however. Although we seem to fall quickly and cheerfully into a workable way of living, Dad is permanently in residence in a part of my brain which ticks off the tasks I need to do to keep him happy, healthy and safe. Enough prunes in cupboard? Tick. What about bourbon biscuits? Tea-bags? Mr Kipling cakes? Tick. Tick. Tick. Paracetamol? Tick. Shaver charged? Tick. Clean towel in bathroom? Tick. Sudocrem for his dry hands? Tick. It's like regressing to having a small child who needs to be fed, watered, shopped for and entertained.

I'd got into a very rackety routine with the girls. Over the last few years, they came and went as they pleased and largely under their own steam. Meal times were usually when we felt like eating, but now they are dictated by the time the carers visit. If Dad doesn't have breakfast as soon as Laura has been at around 9 a.m., lunch at 1 p.m. and supper by 6.30 p.m., then chaos ensues. The other day I was doing an interview which overran, and I was late starting Dad's supper. He needed the loo which delayed things even further. Then Rebecca appeared to get him ready for bed just as Dad was settling down at the dining table. He wasn't pleased to be hauled off to the bathroom to get into his pyjamas when he'd been looking forward to tucking into shepherd's pie. He finally ate at 7.30 p.m. in his pyjamas and dressing gown.

Dad is at the beating heart of a real family. I've always been a sucker for big, noisy families. It's what happens when you arrive at the fag end of a large family, as I did, and listen to your siblings swopping stories about the fun they had, the games they played, the mischief they got up to – all before you arrived. My mother had my sister and two brothers in quick succession – with just a two-year gap in between each. I arrived eight years later. When I was four, Dad, by then a captain in the Army Education Corps teaching soldiers maths, was posted to Germany for a few years. My parents were passionate about education: Dad, because he had left school at fourteen without any qualifications; and Mum, because she could have gone to university and always felt cross with herself for wasting her opportunities. So Hilary, aged fifteen, Simon, thirteen, and Andy, eleven, were all enrolled in boarding schools. Apart from school holidays, we never lived together as a family again.

When I met Richard, I was convinced I'd be able to create my dream at last. I wanted the same loving environment for my girls that Mum and Dad had provided for me and my siblings – but I also wanted the joyful chaos that went with it. Sadly, while Richard and I had the perfect rambling family house – six bedrooms, wood-burning stove in the family room, claw-foot Victorian bath, Aga in the kitchen – we didn't have the rumbustious family life to go with it.

I met Richard in May 1996 at a dinner party thrown by my friend Mary, who had shared my desk as a feature writer on the *Sun*. Mary and Richard had been friends for over ten years, ever since he'd dated another of her friends. That relationship had ended but their friendship had endured. I'd heard a lot about him. I knew he was a city broker, very driven and very successful. I knew that he was recently divorced after a brief marriage. I knew that he had no children. I knew he had suffered a medical trauma of sorts, details of which there is no need for me to go into here; but it was relevant to how our relationship developed. Daft, maybe, but before we'd even met, the fact he'd been through tough times touched my heart.

And then, five years later, we were finally introduced. Hot, bothered and half an hour late because it had been so difficult for the taxi driver to find the flat in London's trendy Docklands, where new streets were springing up like dandelions, I burst into the room with a red face, damp armpits and a rush of apologies, and Richard claimed, despite it all, his heart flipped over. I noticed his periwinkle-blue eyes – so like my dad's – the thick, wavy brown hair flecked with grey which gave him an air of instant gravitas, and the boyish physique which came from a mixture of iron self-discipline and hours in the gym. I fancied him immediately and in the same instant decided he would never be interested in a divorced mother of two with stretch marks and enough baggage to fill the British Rail lost-luggage department. It was a large dinner party so we didn't get to talk very much, but, totally by chance, I'd planned to meet up with my old university friend Bridget the next day to see an exhibition of Eve Arnold's photographs at the Barbican, where Richard had a flat.

'Why don't you and Mary come for coffee first?' he said as he left that night to walk home. So we did. *The Archers* was on in the background, sun was flooding the stylishly minimalist flat and Richard looked even more attractive than the night before in jeans and a simple button-down shirt.

But any frisson of interest I had was instantly quelled as his lips brushed my cheek in greeting and he announced, 'Hello, Sarah.' If he couldn't even remember my name, he couldn't possibly be interested in me. When we said good-bye outside the gallery, I never expected to see him again.

So I was totally unprepared when, a few days later, Mary rang to say that Richard had asked for my phone number. 'I told him that I'd play God,' she said grandly. 'I'll give you his phone number, then it's up to you whether you ring or not.'

'But he couldn't even remember my name!' I cried. 'How on earth can he be interested?'

'Oh, that,' Mary laughed. 'He was just so flustered and nervous.'

I'd like to say I retained my cool. But I didn't. I scribbled both his home and work numbers down with indecent haste on the first thing that came to hand – an old British Telecom bill. I've still got it. It's a talisman I can't bear to part with because, whatever happened later, our relationship began with such passion, such joy and such hope. Chucking out that crunched-up bit of paper would be as mindlessly destructive as gouging his face out of our wedding photos. Whatever I feel now, I don't want to lose sight of how I felt then and how perfect everything once was.

Our first date was at Quaglino's, newly opened by Terence Conran in Mayfair. Tables were hard to come by, so going there on a first date was a huge deal. It was a stickily hot day and I was wearing a cream linen dress and a Georgina van Etzdorf silk scarf. I was so keen to do this right that I'd spent my lunch hour (I was doing shifts at *Best* magazine) speed-reading a book on body language in the local Waterstones so that I'd make sure I gave out the right signals to demonstrate I was perfect girlfriend material. Mirror the way he's sitting to show you're in sync. Keep your arms uncrossed to show you're open and interested. When he's talking, keep your eyes fixed on his. There were pages of the stuff to digest. I'd only been divorced a year, but it seemed aeons since I'd been on a date.

My first husband and I had met at a drunken party in 1983 when I was twenty-five and he was thirty, and, although it took us seven years to get married, I think we both realized as soon as the deed was done – Phillipa Lepley bridal gown from Liberty, church service, choir singing 'Jerusalem' – that it was a mistake. The simple truth was that we got married only because we couldn't think of a good enough reason not to. Even now I can't think of a nobler explanation, and, believe me, I've tried.

We rushed on to have children. My body clock; my urgency. Ellen was born eleven months to the day after our wedding, and Elise arrived seventeen months later. And – pretty inevitably – they didn't bring us closer together. They just made us both face up rather fast to how terribly wrong things were. Once you love somebody body and soul, you know just how sad an imitation it is when you love somebody almost but not quite. When the girls arrived, I knew that I loved them with an ardour I didn't come close to feeling for my husband. And he could see it. We argued viciously and when the rows became really bad, we both realized it was time to end things – and fast.

We separated just before Ellen's third birthday. There are photos of me and the girls in my parents' garden, hunched over a clown-face birthday cake, with me looking so stunned and grief-stricken I could be at a funeral. And that's how it felt. I was consumed by guilt at what I'd done to the girls and how they'd manage without a father, and terror at how I'd cope – alone for virtually the first time in my adult life. To make things even worse, in the traumatic time between separating and divorcing, my mother died, very quickly, of cancer. She was seventy-seven.

So that first date with Richard was like stepping out of darkness into brilliant sunlight. We laughed and chatted so naturally and easily that I didn't need to think once about that daft body-language book. Every look, every smile, every shared confidence screamed out his interest and I couldn't have masked my own if I'd been practising for a hundred years. We both knew it was a momentous date. Richard later admitted shyly that he had kept the bill, while I had rushed out the next day to buy a bottle of Acqua di Gio by Giorgio Armani because it was the perfume I'd sprayed on in the cloakroom that night between courses (Quaglino's was the sort of restaurant that had bottles of designer perfume laid out beside the washbasins for the convenience of the sort of customers who wouldn't dream of stealing them). I wore it virtually every single day until my marriage ended because a single smell transported me back to that table and that moment when I looked laughingly into the eyes of a stranger and knew without knowing how to put it into words that one day we'd be married.

Every step of falling in love was achingly intense because all the time that we were courting, Mary – our friend, our fairy godmother – was dying. She had been diagnosed with inoperable bowel cancer and her determination to wring every last ounce of pleasure from the all-too-brief months she had left made us feel even more blessed. We had a life spread out before us – a life we were going to enjoy together. Richard's tender concern, his eagerness to help Mary in any practical way he could, convinced me what a lovely man he was.

We'd been dating for three months when we went away for a long weekend to a country hotel in Devon. It rained buckets every single day but we didn't care. One afternoon we were sheltering under a tree in our matching kagouls, purchased in dire need that morning, when the most perfect rainbow appeared. It seemed to cover the entire sky, the colours iridescent. Rain dripped off our hoods and splashed down our faces as we kissed.

It was that night, while he was in the bath and I was sitting watching him, that Richard suddenly turned serious. Shyly, he told me about his previous relationship and why he finished it. I was grateful that he trusted me enough to tell me all the details, and impressed that he couldn't bear to have a secret from me.

The girls took to Richard very quickly. He played

hide-and-seek, he read Noddy stories and – best of all – he went through their toy box and patiently and methodically performed emergency surgery on everything from the miniature plastic pony that had lost its tail to the Polly Pocket with only one leg. Nothing seemed to faze him. Nothing embarrassed him. He let the girls dress him up as a baby in a makeshift bonnet and put him to bed, where they sung him lullabies. He uncomplainingly plodded around John Lewis with me as I shopped for a fairy outfit for Ellen's fifth birthday that August. He even helped make the jellies for her party. And everything he fixed for my girls and everything he did with my girls made me love him even more.

To be fair, I hadn't expected the girls to be hard to please. Richard went out of his way to be kind to them and I was undoubtedly a much nicer, calmer mother because I was so happy. Besides, they wanted to be like all their friends and have a father figure around. Sadly, by now, visits from their own father were already tailing off.

Dad was a different matter. I feared he would be worried about my rushing into another relationship. Richard – visiting for the weekend and dressed in shorts, T-shirt and wellington boots – was mowing my lawn when Dad called round. He beamed approvingly. Dad's always been impressed by practical men. Dad, being Dad, didn't lose any time in joshing Richard.

'Are you a farmer's boy?' he asked. Richard looked confused but smiled gamely.

Dad pointed to Richard's Hunter wellies. 'I've never seen

anyone mow a lawn in shorts and wellies before,' he laughed.

Five minutes later, they were deep in conversation about slug pellets and compost heaps.

A few days later, when Dad came round for coffee, I asked him what he thought of Richard.

'He seems a fine chap with a good head on his shoulders and obviously not scared of a bit of hard work.'

This was the point at which I felt I should own up to Dad that Richard was divorced. As he was a dyed-in-the-wool Catholic, I wasn't sure how he would take this.

'Dad, there's something I want you to know. It doesn't matter to me, but it might to you. Richard's been married before. It wasn't for long, and he doesn't have any children, but I know you might not be happy with it.'

Dad looked surprised. 'Why should that bother me? Everybody's allowed a second chance,' he said.

I didn't need Dad's approbation. I was sure enough of my feelings, but when Dad declared Richard a 'fine chap' – his highest form of praise – I was hugely relieved.

Meanwhile, Richard treated Dad with a mixture of affection and respect which endeared him to me even more.

Dad has always prided himself on being a practical, can-do sort of fellow and was desperate for someone to join in the fun of DIY. Richard cheerfully played along. They would spend hours in the garden discussing the best way to mulch leaves or prune the rhododendron bush. It was Dad who instantly noticed and was full of praise when he saw

Richard had painted over the damp patch on my kitchen ceiling.

'Good lad,' he said approvingly. 'I never have understood why anyone would pay to get jobs done round the house when it's such fun getting stuck in yourself.'

I loved the way that although Richard was clearly much more practical than my dear father ever was, he never let Dad realize it. And gosh, was his patience tried. There was the occasion that Dad managed to get all the poles for the girls' new swing mixed up in the time it took Richard to read the instructions. Dad's misguided help was such a hindrance, I wouldn't have blamed Richard for losing his cool. But he never did.

Richard even managed to restrain himself when Dad came round to admire the girls' newly decorated bedroom. Richard had painstakingly papered the walls with a Laura Ashley print of ballerinas and meticulously painted every millimetre of woodwork. It had taken all weekend.

The paint was still wet as Dad charged in. 'Wow. Great job. Is it dry yet?' he said, sticking a large thumb into the paint.

Richard flinched as, you guessed it, Dad's hand came away wet.

'Oops,' said Dad. 'But I guess it won't take two ticks to patch it up?'

'Of course not,' said Richard with a convincing smile, and I wanted to hug him and never let him go.

*

48

Back then, Richard combined quiet self-confidence with a diffidence that I found totally enchanting. He was intelligent, loving, unfailingly good-humoured and totally dependable. He spoiled me with flowers. Every Friday night he'd arrive with a bunch of beautiful roses or lilies, and often a whole salmon from the fishmonger in Leadenhall Market near his office which he would poach for Sunday lunch.

So when he asked me to marry him, in the garden one late Sunday afternoon in September, I didn't hesitate for a second. The girls were thrilled.

'I'm going to die of excitement,' Elise announced dramatically. 'But first I want to know what marrying clothes Richard is going to wear.'

Dad – despite having a Catholic's ingrained disapproval of divorce and remarriage – gave his blessing instantly. 'Nobody should have to live alone. You're a lovely young woman with your life ahead of you and nothing would make me happier than to see you and the girls part of a nice little family again.'

The girls were bridesmaids. When Richard gave them delicate gold bracelets as thank-you presents, Elise wanted to know whether I'd be getting a present too. Ellen piped up quickly: 'Of course not, silly. You've got Richard, haven't you, Mummy? That's your present.'

And that's exactly what he felt like – a totally unexpected gift which had arrived when I most wanted it and least expected it. We married on 8 November 1997 in the Conservatory at the Barbican. I wore an ankle-length embossed-silk column dress in the softest cafe au lait from Monsoon; the girls wore peach frocks with roses in their hair; and when four-year-old Elise – who'd been practising for just this moment ever since she started school two months earlier – sat in front of the registrar and signed her name as one of our witnesses, I thought my heart was going to burst with happiness. We were a family at last.

Dad didn't give me away. As I was thirty-nine and had two daughters in tow, that would have felt decidedly de trop. But I had a very real sense that he was handing me over to be cared for by someone who he was convinced would love me every bit as much as he did and would try every bit as hard as he had always done to protect me and the girls from harm.

We kept the anniversary of every one of our firsts – first meeting, first date, first kiss, first night together. That's how soppy we both were. The fact that Richard also kept other, somewhat more mundane, anniversaries in his diary (left ear syringed) I took as a quirk – just one more thing to love about him.

We carried on living apart for the first sixteen months of our marriage. But eventually the strain of counting the hours until Friday night when we would be together was too much. Richard sold his bachelor flat in the Barbican and, in June 1999, we pooled our resources, stretched our borrowing capacity to the maximum and bought a rambling four-storey town house in Winchester – the quintessential family home.

It seemed that life could not be more perfect. However, looking back now that I've had time to reflect, I think this is precisely when it all started to unravel. The move was a much harder adjustment for Richard than either of us had expected and he began to mourn all the things he had lost. He appreciated how much he had enjoyed the luxury of being able to walk to work. He began to hate the whole business of commuting, the hour stuffed on the train, the smelly tube journey to the office.

I felt guilty. He was only in Winchester because of me. He was the one who had made all the sacrifices, not me. Soon after moving to Winchester, he started talking about giving up his job. I didn't even try and talk him out of it. All that mattered was that he was happy. In fact, we barely discussed it.

I struggle to understand exactly what was going through our brains, because the absolute truth is that we spent more time discussing the merits of green olives over black ones than we did discussing the decision that was to change the course of all our lives so utterly and comprehensively. Still on a post-honeymoon high, I was certain that things would work out. Jobs had always fallen into Richard's lap. He was so practical and hard-working that I imagined he'd easily launch into something else. He was eager to set up a business. And so, in early 2001, he quit his job and started thinking about what to do next.

I tried to be supportive. I loved the idea of Richard being his own boss as much as he did and I admired the way he wasn't driven to make money at any cost. But perhaps that very relaxed attitude should have made us both realize he wasn't cut out to be a businessman. He cringed at the idea of having to sell himself. He didn't want to be desk-bound. He wanted to do something practical, creative and reasonably lucrative. But what?

I loved my career as a writer. I felt fortunate to be earning good money, and I was convinced that Richard would eventually find something and prove a huge success. In the meantime, he cheerfully threw himself into looking after me and the girls and running the house. He did a fantastic job. He ferried the girls to after-school clubs and cheerfully sat through interminable school plays, concerts and ballet productions. He polished their shoes and sewed the badges on their Brownie sashes. When Elise had to dress up as an evacuee for a school project about the Second World War, it was Richard who fashioned her a gas-mask and a label to put around her neck. And when Ellen wanted to dress up as Mildred, the Worst Witch for her school's book week, it was Richard who made her a cloak out of bin liners and a cat out of rags stuffed with newspaper.

He taught the girls how to ride their bikes and how to play Poohsticks. He took them to the hairdresser's and, when the hairdresser discovered they had the dreaded nits, rushed off to buy special shampoo and comforting bars of chocolate. He was a dad in everything but name. Richard was totally content. The girls were a blessing he hadn't expected.

We were both thrilled when Richard found his feet and set himself up as a handyman and gardener. Dad was wild with enthusiasm. If he'd been even five years younger, he'd have begged to join in. Racing around with a lawn mower, hacking down anything that might conceivably have passed for a weed and lighting bonfires (he fervently believed this wasn't just legal but obligatory and had to be carried out at least once a week, preferably when all the neighbours had their washing out), Dad would have been in his element. 'You'll be your own boss, out in the fresh air all day. What could be better?' he said.

The girls were excited, too. That Father's Day, they made Richard a cake and decorated it with a marzipan figure of a man in wellington boots pushing a lawnmower. It was their idea, their surprise.

Richard thought up a name for the business: 'Home and Garden Maintenance'. He put adverts in the local paper and had business cards and flyers printed on classy green paper. I was smugly proud of the slogan I'd come up with: 'Let me take the load from your hands.' It encapsulated all that I proudly believed my budding handyman husband had to offer – strength, dependability, reliability. I'd designed it with what I imagined to be his perfect clients in mind: over-stretched executives and single women desperate for a man who was equally at home behind a lawnmower or up a ladder wielding a Black & Decker.

In fact, his first-ever customer was a dear old lady who dragged Richard round to mow her lawn, got him to do her neighbour's garden too and then baulked at the price. Richard came home jangling a pocket of loose change.

'When I explained that I charged ten pounds an hour, she told me that her old gardener charged only seven pounds,' he said ruefully.

'And what did you say?' I asked.

'Nothing,' Richard admitted, somewhat shamefaced. 'She was so nice, how could I argue?'

I wasn't surprised. That was Richard all over. But it didn't really matter because the work started flooding in. Every Friday, when the local paper came out with Richard's advert in it, his mobile phone would ring with new clients. He wasn't earning a huge amount but I was delighted for him.

Working in people's gardens all day was great for Richard, because he wasn't as sociable as me. And, as often happens with couples, gradually I became less sociable, too. In hindsight, of course, I should have kept up my contact with friends and continued doing all the things that made me happy, such as throwing dinner parties and having friends and family stay for the weekend, while at the same time respecting that Richard was less inclined to want to see people. He very much enjoyed his own company at home. All I can suggest is that when you're in a relationship, you don't know when the act of compromise stops being healthy and becomes misguided.

Getting into the habit of socializing again after Richard left was daunting. I'd lost the knack and, moreover, I felt cripplingly embarrassed. Here I was, a single woman in my fifties, and I felt like a pariah.

One day, Dad was reminiscing about dancing. He talks about the joyful times in his life so often that I'd heard this same story countless times before. I sipped my tea and prepared to zone out. But, as Dad's smile grew broader, I found myself drawn in by his enthusiasm.

'You remember when I moved to Winchester, I didn't know anyone and, if I'm honest, I was a bit lonely without Mum,' Dad said. 'I decided to go along to the Conservative Club because I thought they might have some snooker. I walked in and there was a tea dance in progress. It turned out this happened every Wednesday afternoon. And I couldn't have been made to feel more welcome if I'd been Cary Grant. There were all these lovely young ladies – some only in their late sixties. They wouldn't let me leave until I'd had a dance – with all of them. And they made me promise to come back the next week.'

I remembered how flabbergasted I'd been when Dad first told me about this. It's not simply that he's virtually stone-deaf. He's also so tone-deaf that you need to clap your hands over your ears if he ever threatens to sing. The thought of him gliding around a dance floor, keeping any sort of time to the music, seemed totally surreal. I don't remember my parents ever dancing. And the only occasions on which Dad would dance when I was growing up were when he was trying to tease us. Then he'd fling his arms around like a geriatric Mick Jagger and announce: 'This really sends me' – an expression which he heard some time in around 1966 and has refused to forget. He still does it whenever my girls tell him that they are going to a gig.

'But why, at the grand old age of eighty-six, did you decide to go dancing, Dad?' I asked, remembering how he had taken up private lessons to perfect his new skill and invested in proper dancing shoes.

'I always wanted to learn, but Mum wasn't keen,' he said – and he said it in a way that wasn't at all critical. Unlike Dad, who doesn't seem to know the meaning of the word, Mum was too shy to be sociable. Although she would take on anyone from head teachers to overbearing council officials if she thought they were wrong, she hated attracting attention to herself. In fact, the thought of my somewhat stiff mum being whisked around the dance floor by Dad was frankly farcical.

So, while Mum was alive, Dad happily did all the things she enjoyed. They went to church, played bridge and helped raise money for CAFOD, the Catholic charity set up to help the world's poor. As for hobbies – although they would probably have called them 'interests' – Dad played golf and did his landscape painting and Mum sewed. Dad is slap-dash, but Mum had a strong perfectionist streak and was good at everything she set her mind to. She made all her own clothes and most of mine, my nieces' and my girls' too. Her treat was a trip to the Liberty sale, when she would buy armloads of Tana Lawn cottons.

'You see, Tetty, love,' Dad said, using the pet name he's

called me ever since I was a little girl, 'When Mum died, I had to find my own life.'

As I listened to Dad, I realized that he wasn't just talking about himself, he was talking about me as well. And it dawned on me that he was right. Somehow I had to find the courage to make my own life. But where to start?

It's a week later, and I'm walking Milo with my friend Nicky. 'I've joined a book club,' she says. 'It's great fun. How about coming along with me?'

I'm taken aback. Like Mum, I've always shied away from joining groups. But now seems the right time to bite back my shyness.

'I'd love to,' I say.

Nicky grins. 'And we're also thinking of branching out into Zumba dancing – there's a class at the sports club.'

'Wow,' I say. 'Count me in.' I've no idea what Zumba dancing is – and I may live to regret it – but what have I got to lose? I can't believe all the new possibilities that are opening up in the space of fifteen seconds.

When I tell Dad, he smiles encouragingly. 'Well done.' Then his face takes on a slightly perplexed look. 'Incidentally, what exactly is a book club?'

THREE

LIFE'S TOO SHORT TO
WORRY ABOUT DYING

I realized something truly remarkable today. I can't remember the last time I thought about death or, more specifically, about me dying. Horribly. Of cancer. For almost three years it's been the first thing I've thought about when I wake up in the morning and the last thing I've thought about before I've gone to sleep. I made this discovery when Dad and I were having our mid-morning cup of coffee. We've got into a bit of a routine now. It's surprisingly comforting. When I hear the click of the front door that announces Laura's arrival, I give myself fifteen self-indulgent minutes with the *Today* programme before going downstairs to make Dad's breakfast. It's always the same – one bowl of milky porridge, one of prunes, a cup of tea, two aspirins and 10ml of laxative.

Then I work in my office next door to Dad's room while he snoozes in his chair before reconvening for elevenses and a brief chat. Mostly, Dad chooses the topic. I'm learning that he likes telling stories that he's familiar with and that conjure up happy memories. And he doesn't welcome questions or comments – they interrupt his flow and confuse him, jolting him back to a present he'd rather be absent from. But today I ask to hear the drowning story. I know my own version – I've lived with it for forty-five years and it's shaped the person I am. But I don't remember Dad ever telling me his account.

'You were eight years old and Mum and I had taken you to the seaside – a little place in the New Forest called Lepe,' he begins. 'You were happily playing with some other girls and boys. You were on a shallow sandbank, which was fine, because you didn't really know how to swim. But I seem to remember that you were scared of seaweed and when you found your feet getting tangled in it, you tried to get away. You ended up falling right off the sandbank and suddenly you were in deep water. There was no warning sign.

'I saw you waving to me so I waved back. Then, suddenly, I realized that you weren't waving at all but crying out for help. I've never had to react so quickly in my life. Mum wasn't around – she'd gone off to the car to get her cigarettes. I pulled off my trousers and shoes – there was no time to get my shirt unbuttoned – and jumped in. I was up to my neck in water in seconds. It was deep and the tide was going out. I don't know how long it was before I reached you. But I got you safe. I was holding you in one arm, swimming with the other and trying to get you to swim too with your free arm. I was telling you: "Forward. Back. Up."

'I lost track of time. You were only a little thing but, swimming with you all that way against the tide, I was absolutely whacked. As I was coming in to shore, a number of people suddenly appeared. They clapped and one lady rushed over and said: "Give her to me." Then I stood up and tried to wade ashore, but I was so exhausted that I collapsed face down in the water. I would have drowned, but some men saw what was happening. They waded out to me. One of them was an off-duty policeman – he knew what to do. He gave me mouth-to-mouth resuscitation. Those chaps saved my life. There was a flash in my head and a big bang as the air came into my lungs and I was back in the land of the living.

'I could see that I was being held up by these two chaps, one on either side.

'"I'm so sorry. I must have fainted in the sun," I said.

'They looked at me. "No," they said. "Look, you're soaking wet. You swam out and saved the little girl."

'"Did I?" I asked. And then it came back to me. And I was so shocked and so relieved.

'When poor Mum appeared, she saw me on the beach all grey and thought I was dying. But I'd saved you. If I hadn't – well, I'd have had to emigrate to Australia. I could never have lived with Mum again and the shame of not having been able to rescue you.'

It was strange to see 'my story' through Dad's eyes. I remember feeling terror, desperation when Dad didn't seem to understand I needed him, then accepting that I was going to die. I'd been reading *Jo's Boys*, one of Louisa M. Alcott's sequels to *Little Women*. One of the characters meets 'a watery grave' at sea. The line had stuck in my head. As I was swept further and further out to sea I kept repeating those melodramatic words, which somehow gave me comfort.

But what I'd never fully appreciated was Dad's quiet bravery. I dug around in Dad's drawer to find the medal I'd made for him when we were released from hospital later that day. There it was among the pile of paracetamol tablets, hearing-aid batteries and handkerchiefs. It was a little St Christopher which I'd stitched higgledy-piggledy on to a blue cloth. I remember Dad lying in bed, pale and greyish. I'm not sure I'd ever seen him in bed before. He was always up first, crashing around, urging Mum to finish her cup of tea from the Teasmade and get up too. I pinned it on to his pyjama jacket and kissed him; but had I ever thanked him properly? Had I ever really understood the courage it takes to face down death and then move seamlessly on with life? Dad never spoke about what he had done, never asked for or expected anything in return from me. Even when I was a horrible, swaggering, know-it-all teenager, he never dreamt of cutting me down to size by reminding me how much I owed him.

My daddy, my wonderful strong daddy, who really was prepared to give up his life for me. And who almost did. Even now, in this very last stage of his life when he knows death is stalking him, he's so strong-minded, so stoic. He has a frank but unfearful attitude to death.

How does he do it? When death threatened to come calling for me, I collapsed.

Virtually from the moment I've had them, my breasts have been causing problems with one lump after another. I had my first cancer scare when I was twenty-five. A visit to the doctor for an examination led to a hospital check-up, a mammogram and the very real fear that – young as I was – I might have breast cancer.

Five years later, I had two tiny lumps removed from my left breast. Although the consultant assured me that this was purely a precautionary measure, I was still frightened.

There was another scare in 1993 as my first marriage was breaking up. Another in 2000, and yet another in 2005. Each time, I found a lump, went to the doctor, and set in motion a nerve-wracking round of examinations. Each time, I'd expected to be reassured that nothing was wrong. Instead, even the doctor couldn't decipher what was going on in my breasts without tests. I became convinced that I would never be able to tell whether a lump was cancerous or not.

And I was suffused with embarrassment at wasting so much of the doctors' time and so many medical resources. I'd been schooled by a mother who was so respectful of doctors that she believed anything short of a heart attack was too trivial to bother them with.

In fact, scrap that. Even when Dad did have a heart attack, apparently she wouldn't believe him at first. 'But you haven't got a pain in your chest,' she would have said while he writhed on the bedroom floor in the middle of the night, complaining of shooting pains in his arm. I wasn't there, of course – I was living in London – but I can imagine this is how it went until, finally, Dad looked ill enough for Mum to call an ambulance.

However, my run-ins with phantom lumps also made me wary of checking my breasts for fear of sparking off yet another round of 'cry wolf' and so, when I felt a tiny lump in my right breast as I was in the bath one evening in December 2006, I told myself this was yet another false alarm. And yet, just like you know without a shadow of a doubt that you are in love, I knew this lump was different. It wasn't even the size of a petit pois. But it was hard and intractable. Somehow it felt different from all the others. I made Richard feel it.

'If you're worried, you must go to the doctor, darling. But I can't feel anything,' he said.

I didn't want to go to the doctor. I'd done that often enough and I didn't want to go through all that fear and then end up feeling foolish yet again. Instead, every day or two, I'd check my breast, hoping that I'd imagined the lump or that it would have vanished. It was always there.

Then a woman in my weekly Italian class was diagnosed with breast cancer. Suddenly, the issue seemed more real. So, in February, I went to the doctor. He was a terribly sweet, terribly solicitous young man, barely out of medical school. He couldn't be sure what the lump was. In fact, at first he couldn't even find it. So he arranged for a hospital appointment. 'Just to be on the safe side, I'll mark it urgent so you will be seen within two weeks. The checks are there. Let's use them,' he said. Actually, that didn't make me feel at all safe. I just felt I was starting down a path knowing I didn't like the look of the way ahead. Richard was away for the week, working on a client's property in the Caribbean. I told him as soon as he got home.

He was terribly concerned. 'If you're worried, let me ring the doctor and see if we can get you a private appointment and be seen more quickly. You mustn't hang around,' he said, which made me even more worried.

We had a half-term holiday planned in Madrid with the girls and Dad the following week. I wasn't prepared to disrupt that. In fact, I was so determined not to acknowledge any sense of urgency that I even postponed my hospital appointment by two days to accommodate our return flight. But cancer stalked me. As we drove from the airport to our apartment, virtually the first thing I saw was a mobile breast-scanning unit. I wished to God I hadn't seen it. But I had and I couldn't forget the omen.

Back home, nine days later, the young registrar in the Royal Hampshire County Hospital's breast unit was examining my breast with an ultrasound scanner. The last time I'd seen one of those was when I'd been heavily pregnant. Now the sonar waves were showing up a solid lump.

'Could it be a cyst?' I asked.

She looked suddenly solemn. 'Cysts don't normally show up on ultrasounds.' And that was the moment I knew. Cancer had always seemed both impossible and utterly inevitable. And now here it was. What followed over the next few weeks were grains of tiny, distracting comfort which I grabbed hold of like precious talismans. But from that second, deep down, I knew that this was different – this was real.

I don't know whether Richard knew it too. I don't even remember what he said. I just remember feeling absolutely sure that he would know what to do. He would understand what was involved and he would be strong for me. I was virtually catatonic as he drove me home, via Sainsbury's, knowing instinctively that I needed something, anything, to take my mind off things. 'We can get the holiday photos from Madrid developed,' he said, clutching for a scrap of normality. But nothing was normal any more.

In the vegetable aisle, after dropping off the photos, an elderly couple were squabbling over which tomatoes to buy. Small? Large? Why on earth did they care? I wanted to shake them. I loathed them for being alive and for bothering about anything so mind-numbingly stupid. They were so much older than me, yet they were healthy and I wasn't. 'Don't you know how lucky you are?' I wanted to scream.

Looking at the photos was surreal. I searched my image for traces of illness. I certainly looked thin. But did I look ill? Did I look as though I had cancer? Does anyone ever look as though they have cancer?

The following day I'd been booked in for a core biopsy. Under local anaesthetic, a tiny sample of tissue was taken from the lump. The radiologist was pale-skinned and red-haired, like me. Maybe that's why I warmed to her instantly. That and her kindness. When she told me the lump was tiny, I looked in her face, searching for clues. Could I really believe her?

'I can't tell a lie to save my life,' she said, as she prepared to extract cells from the lump. 'Honestly, it's tiny – about two centimetres. If it *is* cancer, it's not been there long. But, biopsies aren't a hundred per cent accurate. If it were me, even if the result comes back clear, I'd get the lump removed just to be on the safe side.'

It was the best piece of advice, because, sure enough, two days later I was sitting in front of the consultant as he was explaining that the biopsy had indeed come back clear. Tall, rangy, with greying hair, delicate hands and an air of quiet authority, Dick Rainsbury was my idea of the perfect consultant. But even he didn't have all the answers. Were there no cancer cells to be found, or had the needle simply missed them? Mr Rainsbury didn't know. He offered me the choice of waiting to see if the lump got bigger or having it removed as soon as possible.

'I'd like to get rid of it,' I said. So the operation was booked for two weeks' time – 15 March.

As Richard put his arm around me and led me gently out of the room, it was impossible not to think about Mum. She had learnt that she had cancer on her seventy-seventh birthday in October 1994. She'd been having problems swallowing for several months but was convinced she had a hiatus hernia. When the drugs didn't work, the GP had arranged for her to have a scan. No one on her side of the family had ever suffered from cancer, and Mum was so gung-ho about the whole thing that she walked over to the surgery alone to pick up the results. I'd never wanted to imagine how shocked and terrified she must have been when the doctor told her she had cancer. Without even my dad to lean on, she must have felt so alone.

I tried not to remember how desperately frail she had become in the terrible months that followed. I tried not to think about her yellow skin, her glazed eyes, her distended stomach, and how, in those last few days, she had begged for more morphine to take away the pain.

It was a totally different form of cancer – but would it be a different outcome? After Mum died, I rarely felt the need to talk to her. It wasn't that I didn't love her and miss her. I did, desperately. But she was so much a part of me, and me of her, that I knew what she would think and say in most situations. She was alive in every beat of my heart. But now I was faced with something we'd never discussed: death. I repeated over and over again: 'Mummy, you've been here. You've done it. Help me to be as strong as you.'

I told the girls that I was having a tiny operation on my breast, but we decided not to tell anyone else. After all, there was nothing to worry about, was there? I emailed friends, airily explaining: 'I'm having minor surgery.' I told work colleagues the same. Who cared if everyone thought I'd got a bunion or ingrowing toenails? I'd tell them the truth when it was all over. And, as I got sucked back into the routine of life, I was almost able to convince myself that this was yet another false alarm in a long history of them.

The operation itself was a breeze. I was in and out within the day. And then I waited for the results. I thought I was calm. But, actually, I can't really have been calm, because the evening before I was due to get the results, Richard and I had a hideous row. We'd driven Ellen, who was in the Hampshire Youth Choir, to a concert. I had suggested that while Ellen was singing we could have a meal out. It would be a treat. We drove around for ages in the little country villages around Cosham, desperately trying to find somewhere to eat. Neither of us was in a great mood when we finally found a reasonable-looking wine bar.

If I'm honest, I longed to be looked after, to be treated, like I had been at the beginning of our relationship, when Richard had taken me and the girls on trips to the theatre, restaurants and galleries. 'Our' restaurant had been a wonderful Indian around the corner from the Barbican. On weekends when we lived apart, I'd often bring the girls up to Richard's flat for the weekend. Our first port of call, straight from the station, was always the Smithfield Tandoori. It was Richard's stamping ground, Richard's treat.

The truth for me was that I had slipped into the role of

major wage earner without ever looking for it or wanting it. And – as much as I admired the fact that Richard, like my dad, wasn't remotely mercenary – sometimes I longed for us to have a more equal relationship. I thought of my parents. Dad kept the family afloat singlehandedly all through my childhood.

It was only when Dad finally left the army to go into teaching in a secondary school that Mum had the chance to work. And, with Dad's support, she grabbed it. She was forty-eight when she trained as a teacher – and she celebrated becoming a grandma the same week she took her final exams.

Dad was hugely proud of Mum and her career. But he certainly didn't see it as the chance to take a back seat. In fact, he was so keen to keep working and stay busy that he was still doing odd months as a supply teacher when he was well into his seventies.

I didn't want to replicate my parents' relationship but being the wage-earner, calling the shots, wasn't a role I particularly liked and certainly not one I wanted to nurture. Over the years, Richard had dovetailed his behaviour to mine, becoming increasingly laid-back. But recently he wasn't just laid-back, he appeared disinterested.

I hadn't expected him to earn a mint from gardening. Money wasn't the issue. What I wanted was for him to enjoy his job.

I looked back to how enthusiastic and excited he had

been when he first started his business. What had happened to make him now seem so disenchanted? I couldn't understand it.

A few glasses of rioja at the wine bar and fear about the impending results the next day contributed to the simmering resentment that flared up when I suggested that, as work tailed off over the winter, Richard should put an advert for his business in the local paper.

'I've done that before,' he said, pouring himself another glass of wine. 'It didn't work.'

'That was two months ago,' I reminded him, through gritted teeth. 'Why don't you try again?'

'It's expensive. I don't have the money,' he said, shrugging.

'But it's worth it – how else are you going to get new clients?'

'OK, OK. Just stop nagging,' he moaned. 'It's my business and I know what I'm doing.'

And that was it. It made me so sad and angry. I couldn't help but think of the way Richard used to be, when he would have countered enthusiastically with new ideas. Now it was as if he didn't care much about the business or what I thought about him.

'Aren't you going to say anything?' I demanded.

He shrugged again. 'What is there to say? You're so upset. Whatever I say will make it worse.'

So he didn't say anything. And neither did I. We collected

Ellen from the concert and drove home in silence. For the first time in our marriage, I spent the night in the spare room. But I was too miserable to sleep. I'd run out of ideas about how to make myself happy, how to help Richard to be happier when nothing seemed to make him smile anymore. I wondered how on earth we'd got here when we'd both believed so adamantly that we could make it work forever. Was this just the end of the beginning – that period that is so ridiculously, outrageously blissful that you'd die of emotional exhaustion if it lasted forever? Or was this the beginning of the end? Were we going to limp on like this?

I was still so angry with Richard the next morning that I almost went to the hospital without him. But I was also scared enough not to want to be alone, so he was with me when – an hour late – I was finally called in to see Mr Rainsbury. By then I was only thinking of one thing – the phone interview I had lined up with Dame Kelly Holmes, the Olympic winner, in thirty minutes' time. So I was eager to be given the all-clear and get home as soon as possible.

As soon as Mr Rainsbury opened his mouth, I knew that he wasn't reading from the script I'd expected. My insignificant, inconsequential lump was cancerous. Peering at me over his glasses, he said: 'We were right to remove it. It was a tumour.' My head was reeling as I tried to concentrate and sift the truly terrible news from the slightly less terrible.

My tumour was Grade 2 – cancers vary from Grade 1 (virtually imperceptible) to Grade 3 (advanced). It was oestrogen-receptor positive – which meant the drug Tamox-ifen would help long-term. Suddenly we were talking about dates for more radical surgery – to remove all the tissue around the lump. But my brain was still in the past where my body was fit and healthy and I couldn't keep up.

How do you react when you hear the words you've most feared? I went into super gracious mode. As Mr Rainsbury suggested operating in six days' time – on 4 April – I acted as though I'd been invited to tea by the Queen. 'That sounds perfect,' I nodded, pen poised over my diary page, as though I was making a social engagement. My voice had the stran-gulated cut-glass vowels Mum's had had whenever she an-swered the phone. How are people supposed to behave when told they have cancer? If there were rules, I hadn't learnt them. I didn't think I'd ever need them. I wasn't going to let anyone – least of all me – know just how petrified I was. I was yet to discover that life was never, ever going to be the old brand of normal again.

Once outside, I cried and howled. I only stopped long enough to interview Kelly Holmes. It was the last work I'd do for almost a year. Back home I couldn't sit still. I paced up and down, made endless cups of tea I didn't drink, grabbed newspapers I couldn't read. Just three minutes alone in one place was long enough for my brain to start tearing me apart with terror. And then there was the telling everyone. I wanted to put it off forever. If people didn't know, I could pretend this hadn't happened. There was no way I could put the words 'breast' and 'cancer' in the same sentence without bursting into tears. I was terrified of people's reactions – not that I'd frighten them, I was too selfish to care about that, but that they would frighten me by betraying alarm. My nerves were stripped bare. Richard made the phone calls. I couldn't even bear to be in the same room. What if a scintilla of fear crept into his voice? I needed him to be strong. I needed him to believe everything was going to be OK so that I could be, too.

I needed him with a passion and a desperation that left me aching with vulnerability. I clung to him that first sleepless night. If I could have crawled into his body for safe-keeping, I would have done. I completely forgot all the annoyances and irritations of the last few years. Or, if I remembered them, I berated myself for having carped at him, for not treasuring this precious relationship, this wonderful man. Because, most of all, I needed all those things I'd fallen in love with – his dependability, his loyalty, his calmness and his quiet confidence – to get me through this.

I must have told Richard a hundred times a day that I loved him. His favourite response when I asked him if I'd be OK was to point to his head. 'It's all down to what's in here,' he said. I wanted to believe him. After all, he had his own experience of dealing with ill health, and I hung pathetically on his every word as though he knew best, as though he could save me – although I'm not sure I actually believed in mind over matter. It was too trite, too facile and didn't take account of the thousands of people every year who fight cancer with every inch of resolution in their body and still die.

I knew I had to be the one to tell the girls. I put it off for three days – long enough, I hoped, to be able to do it without betraying my terror that I might be leaving them. I was angry and bitter that cancer should hit me now. Ellen was sitting her GCSEs; Elise had SATs exams. What would this do to them? I tried to be upbeat, but it was a total act.

'When I had that little operation, the doctor found a lump in my breast. It's cancer. But it's tiny, and it's been caught very early. There's nothing to worry about,' I said, willing myself to believe the lie. They rushed to hug me and that's when I started crying.

'I love you so much,' I whispered.

I had the operation to remove the lump and the lymph nodes in my right armpit three days before Easter. I'd almost talked myself into believing that the lump really was as inconsequential as I was telling everyone. Getting rid of the lymph nodes was purely precautionary.

The last thing I remember was chatting to the anaesthetist. 'Think of something nice,' he said, smiling down at me. I thought of my girls.

I was home the next day, sore and groggy. I was told I'd have to wait a week for the results of the findings from the operation. Easter passed in a haze. All day, every day, all I could think about was the test results. During that last hour in the waiting room (the surgeon was backlogged), I was so on edge that it would have taken a horse tranquillizer to calm me down. And then I was sitting in front of the consultant – a stranger who wasn't Mr Rainsbury – and he was telling me that the cancer had spread. My breast was a tissue of stray cancer cells. Even worse, the cancer had spread out of my breast. It had reached two of my lymph nodes. Left alone, it would soon be tearing through my whole body. The only way to try and eradicate the cancer was to remove my entire breast. I would have to have a mastectomy. Urgently.

I thought I'd prepared myself for bad news, but this was beyond my worst imaginings. All the air had been sucked out of me. I couldn't breathe. I wept on the nurse as I undressed to be examined by the consultant: 'I've got two little girls. I can't die.' There was nothing she could say, so she just patted my back. In my diseased, cancer-riddled body I had never felt more alone or more terrified. My body, known only to me, was suddenly alien. Strangers knew the most intimate things about my body, were making diagnoses and decisions. Where had I gone? What was left of me?

The consultant started drawing pencil pictures of how he could reconstruct my breast. I felt so sick with shock that I couldn't look. I just kept nodding like a stupid nodding dog. Richard squeezed my hand. But his mouth was clenched tight. His eyes were swimming and I knew he hadn't expected this either. I was going to be very sick and would almost certainly lose not just a breast but all my hair. I was at the start of a very long journey and I didn't know if I had the strength to make it to the end.

I'd dipped my toes into a harmless-looking pool and suddenly I was being sucked deeper and deeper into a hideous swamp. How much blacker could this get? If cancer was possible, if cancer in the lymph nodes was possible, what other nameless horrors lay out there? I tried to calm myself with the words Mum used in a crisis, words from a prayer by the mystic Julian of Norwich: 'All shall be well, all shall be well, and all manner of things shall be well.' They helped me down from the brink of terror but only for a few minutes.

There was no easy way to tell people. Once again, I left it to Richard. Just like Mum, I'd been so determinedly gung-ho that everyone was as shocked as I was. How I wished I'd been less positive – and better prepared. Telling the girls was hardest of all. I'd assured them this was just a blip. They were terribly quiet. Later, upstairs, I heard them crying. I wanted to run to them. But I was crying, too.

Almost as great as the terror of cancer was the terror of losing control. If I didn't get a grip, I'd go under. It was like forcing a runaway train back on to the track. There's a film, *Unstoppable*, which I saw after I recovered. The train is careering to disaster and only two men can stop it – a rookie driver (Chris Pine) and an old-timer (Denzel Washington). It's edge-of-the seat stuff as they race against the clock to avert tragedy. That's how I felt. The mental energy of keeping myself focused was exhausting.

After my marriage to Richard ended, I had to do it all over again. I was sent reeling back into that same state of shock. It was like looking at the world from behind a shop window. Normal life was going on outside but I was trapped behind the plate glass. I was petrified that the shock and stress would set the cancer off again. My brain went round and round in circles. Anger and fear propelled each other. I found distractions, just as I'd done when I was ill. I watched hour after hour of *Desperate Housewives*, *The West Wing* and *The Sopranos* – anything to take my mind off the same well-worn track. I went for long walks. I played badminton ferociously three times a week.

But nothing did me quite as much good as having Dad here. It's wonderful to share your life with someone who always has your best interests at heart, who will love you however hideously you behave and forgive you whatever you do. Dad is so constant, so reliable, so sanguine, and that calms me. I can't imagine there will ever be a time when he won't greet me with a smile. Mood swings just aren't his style.

As the weeks pass with Dad here, I'm becoming so bound up in the minutiae of caring for him that I don't have the time to think about myself. The gentle routine that makes him feel secure gives me respite from my fears. And, gradually, the major terror – the terror of the cancer coming back – is fading. It's not just down to the fact that I don't have time to think; it's Dad's attitude rubbing off on me.

Before Dad moved in, I was worried that having someone so weak and helpless around would intensify the memories I had of when I was weak and sick. In fact, it's the exact opposite. Helping Dad reminds me of how strong and well I am now. Sometimes the contrast between how young and fit I feel and how frail and fragile he is makes me want to cry.

When I brought his dinner in to him yesterday, I watched him inch his way from his armchair to his dining chair, breathing heavily through the discomfort, with each step his knees creaking like an ancient oak tree in a rainstorm, his face contorted in pain. But when he sat down, he still managed to smile: 'This looks lovely, Tetty. Thank you.'

There's a line I remember from Jane Austen's *Persuasion,* which I read when I was ill. It's when Sophia, Admiral Croft's loyal, loving and wonderfully feisty wife, explains how she copes with the dangers of his job. 'We none of us expect to be in smooth water all our days,' she says. It strikes at the heart of what Anne, the heroine of the novel, is beginning to learn. When she was young she rejected Sophia's brother, a poor sailor. Now she bitterly regrets playing safe and not following her heart.

That's Dad all over. Life is never set fair. Even though his physical abilities are lessening all the time, he accepts it with such grace. Simple things he used to do and enjoy are increasingly beyond him, but Dad is philosophical.

When I was preparing Dad's room, I filled the walls with some of the prints he had chosen with Mum: Picasso's *Portrait of a Woman*, Van Gogh's *Café Terrace at Night*,

The Laughing Cavalier and – above his bed, as it always had been – a pen-and-ink drawing of Michelangelo's *Pietà*, which they had seen together at the Vatican in Rome. I also put up two of my favourite paintings of Dad's, which I hoped would evoke happy memories: a gentle New Forest pony with her foal beside a backdrop of golden trees; and ducks on the lake at Chandler's Ford, where my parents lived for the last twenty years of Mum's life.

Now, at least once a day, Dad gets up close and looks contemplatively at them. 'Not bad,' he mutters with a sense of pride and almost surprise. It's as though he finds it hard to remember that painting was once such a passion and that, considering he was totally untrained, he was rather good at it.

Dad took up painting after he retired. He'd enjoyed sketching as a child and, if he'd been born at a different time or had come from a different background, might well have gone to art school. Instead, he got a 'proper job' with a regular salary and a pension and confined himself to drawing pictures for us, which, Dad being Dad, he would knock off in five minutes flat. One of the first things he did to fill his time after Mum died was to make my girls a doll's house – which he built and painted from scratch.

When he quit teaching, he signed up for painting lessons at his local adult education centre. He rushed along enthusiastically to the first one, but when the teacher wheeled out the exact same vase of dried flowers the following week, he looked at his finished work and decided that he'd learnt enough already. He bought a dressing gown from a Marie Curie charity shop – buying an artist's smock would have seemed pretentious – and a set of oil paints and an easel, which he put up in the kitchen so that he could catch all the natural light. He painted landscapes, usually of local scenes he knew and loved, based on photos with a good splash of imagination. Dad was prolific, knocking off most paintings in a couple of days. He spent the first day on the background – blue skies with scudding clouds were a failsafe. As soon as the paint was dry, he would throw himself into the fun part: horses, sheep, ducks, swans, and even, on one occasion, a moose (photographed on a holiday with my Auntie Mary and her husband in Canada). Dad wasn't remotely precious about his painting but he was surprisingly painstaking.

He carried on with just as much enthusiasm after Mum died. In fact, his waning interest was one of the first signs that he was slowing down. I first noticed it after his ninety-fifth birthday in March 2010. As usual, I'd thrown a party for him and invited the neighbours and all his dancing friends. As she left, his favourite dancing partner, Beryl, admired Dad's painting of New Forest ponies which hung in the entrance hall. Dad had made presents of several different paintings to Beryl over the years and was thrilled to know that this was one she really wanted. He decided to paint a new version especially for her. He had his easel set up by

9 a.m. the next morning to catch the best of the sunlight. But, while the inspiration was there, he couldn't get the horses to look the way he wanted. Days and then weeks went by, and Dad kept returning to the painting. While the background pleased him, he couldn't breathe any life into the horses. He didn't say it and I never guessed, but the truth was that he didn't have the strength and dexterity to control the paintbrush the way he used to. He could still visualize exactly what he wanted, but his skill had ebbed away.

'I'll come back to it another time,' Dad said gamely when I noticed the easel had been put away in the cupboard. He never did. Poor Beryl had to make do with the half-dozen paintings of Dad's she already had.

Dad's view on life is that you have to roll with the punches. And God, has Dad endured some terrible punches. The worst for him – for all of us – was when my sister Hilary died.

When I was ill, I thought about Hilary constantly. It wasn't so much that I felt her presence; I'm not sure that I did. But when I thought of her, I stopped feeling sorry for myself. How could I dare to expect pity when I'd had so much more than she had ever had? She was twenty-six when she died. I was forty-eight when I was diagnosed. Her daughters, Frances and Sibylla, were just four and two. Mine were fifteen and fourteen. If I left them, they would be bereft, but they could cope.

*

Hilary was living in Brussels with her husband, Brian, and the girls. She had met Brian at Oxford. He was at Balliol; she was at St Anne's. They'd fallen giddily in love and married the second they graduated. Brian worked for Reuters and Hilary had just secured a contract with *The Times* to write about education in the heart of the strange new world of the EEC. It was March 1973 and they'd returned to England for the weekend to visit Brian's father in Cambridge, as he was ill. They caught the ferry back to Boulogne. Driving through the countryside, their Renault 2CV crashed into a tree on the side of the road. Hilary wasn't wearing a seat belt. She hit her head with such force that she never recovered consciousness, dying hours later in hospital in Lille.

Dad has rarely talked about losing Hilary. I was in no doubt that it was the worst thing that had ever happened to him or Mum, but I hadn't cared to examine just how deep the scars went. But, as he gets closer to death himself, Dad has begun to talk about Hilary's death. Perhaps it's because, as a devout Catholic, he firmly believes that she and Mum will be waiting for him when he dies.

'It was all so sudden. She was so young – barely more than a child,' Dad says. 'Mum's headmistress rang my school and asked me to come straight over. I didn't know what was going on and I didn't know what to think. I walked into the headmistress's office and Mum was there. She was crying. "There has been an accident, darling." I wanted to comfort her. "It will be all right, love," I said. And then Mum told me: "It's Hilary. She's dead." And I felt my heart stop. Poor Mum: she always had to be truthful and couldn't be delicate.

'Brian, the nanny and the two babies were in the car, but no one else was touched. Mum and I went to France together the next day. Her brain was so badly injured they told us that it was better that she had died.'

I've never seen Dad cry. So it's a shock to see that his eyes are swimming. 'It's the worst thing that's ever happened,' he murmurs so quietly that I can barely hear him.

I think of losing one of my girls like that. I can't imagine how I'd get up the next morning, and every morning after that. I've been engulfed by such anger and bitterness since Richard left, trudging along like a poor, clapped-out pit pony over the same fruitless track, so plagued by 'what ifs' that I can't conceive how I'd manage to steer myself through something so much more tragic, so much more random.

'How did you keep going after Hilary died, Dad?'

'You just have to. You can't ever be so angry that you let it ruin your life and everyone else's.'

'And what about if you are so scared that you don't think you can keep going?'

'Scared of what?' Dad is bemused. And I realize that fear doesn't really enter his vocabulary.

'Death,' I admit, half-embarrassed.

'Death?' Dad looks surprised. 'Why on earth would anyone be so scared of dying that it stops them enjoying life? You can't do anything to avoid dying, but you can do all you can to have a happy life.'

I so hope that he is right. Is it really in my power? Can I really choose to be happy when I have been so frightened and so unhappy for so long?

FOUR

DRESS TO IMPRESS

I'm standing in front of a mirror in Liberty and I'm doing something I've never done before. I'm deciding whether to buy myself a ring. It's a frantically busy Saturday afternoon bang in the middle of the January sales. But as I run the gamut of poses, hand coyly on shoulder, hand defiantly on hip, hand grandly extended in expectation of a kiss, I'm transported into my own little oasis of calm. My gaze slides from the square-cut, multifaceted quartz, the colour of crème de menthe, to my face. My shoulders are thrown back. My eyes are blazing with excitement and there's a confident smile on my lips. I'm a woman happy in her own skin.

It's perhaps not a wildly expensive ring by most people's standards, a fraction of what the average engagement ring costs – £400 reduced to £200 in the sale. But for me it's a wildly extravagant gesture. Totally unpremeditated, totally spur of the moment. I'd never imagined wanting to buy myself a ring until I saw this one. I'm there but not quite. Seeing the hesitation in my eyes – Can I really afford it?

Should I really indulge myself like this? – the girls are egging me on.

'Go for it, Mum,' says Elise. 'You can wear it for ever. You'll never regret it.'

'It's perfect and we know you love it,' Ellen chimes in.

Time's running short. We've left Dad home alone with a sandwich, a barrel of biscuits and a Thermos flask of tea while we've escaped to London. We have to be back for his supper, which means catching a train in forty-five minutes. How do I explain my hesitation? I'm not entirely sure the girls understand – they're too young to have had their hearts broken. And, I hope, too liberated, for a ring to bear the weight of emotion it does for me. They're not children of the seventies, unsettling mixtures of feminism and traditionalism. How can I possibly explain to them – particularly here in the middle of Liberty with an over-solicitous shop assistant hovering in the background – that there was a time when declining to shave your legs was a feminist gesture and when going without a bra was a grandly defiant act, but having holes in your tights was plain slovenly? Because as I toss up whether to shell out or walk away, it's not just about the money. It's about the finger I'm planning to wear the ring on. My wedding finger. I have always loved rings – it's the one piece of jewellery that provides infinite pleasure because you can see it all the time and, if it's dramatic like this one, never forget you are wearing. Maybe I'm weird, but, when I meet a woman for the first time, I always peer at her engagement ring. It can tell you so much about the background story – and what it doesn't tell, you can entertain yourself by conjecturing. Did he choose it? Did she? Was it a week's wages? A month's? Did they ever imagine a time when a dinky flower-shaped diamond jobbie would look out of place on a hand covered in liver spots?

When I got engaged to my first husband in 1985, we had so little money that we ended up scouring second-hand shops for a ring. The one I chose was an art deco design – a minute emerald nestling between two diamond chips. It cost £82. Cheap and unflashy, maybe, but it sealed the biggest commitment of my life. I was so eager to be egalitarian, I insisted on going halves. On honeymoon in India five years later, my proud new husband took me to a jewellery shop in Rajasthan and bought me the most jaw-droppingly exquisite sapphire ring. This time I let him pay.

When Ellen was born just as the sun was setting on a cloudless day in August 1991, he did a victory run around the labour room and then delved into his pocket to find the ring he had bought me to celebrate – a delicately carved Victorian ring mounted with five diamonds. Even the midwife went misty-eyed. In the months that followed as I staggered blearily from bed to feed her, I'd sometimes slip on the ring, look at those diamonds – worth a cool £900 – and feel a surge of utter contentment. A husband, a daughter, a diamond ring. What more could any woman want?

When Elise was born, seventeen months later, my husband marked the event with a ruby ring. I'd look at my rings – one on each hand – and imagine the moment, long in the future, when I'd hand them down. One ring for each beautiful daughter. What a perfect vision. What a sad fantasy. Because, when my marriage ended, I discovered that when love dies, jewellery instantly loses its sparkle. I didn't want to look at those rings because they were a bitter reminder of all the dashed hopes and dreams. And I certainly didn't want to wear them. In fact, I didn't even want them in the house. I auctioned them for a fraction of their worth. Even cashing the cheque a few weeks later made me feel sick.

Growing up, I was never remotely interested in wedding dresses, but I was always transfixed by rings. Perhaps I got my interest from Mum. She had very little jewellery, but what she had was terribly important to her. When my parents got engaged in 1944, finding a jeweller with anything on his shelves was so difficult that Dad ended up buying Mum the meanest of diamond rings. The band was so thin that it wore through even before I was born. After her mother died, Mum took to wearing her engagement ring instead – a stonking blood-red ruby surrounded by diamonds.

But Dad was very keen to buy Mum her own ring – something they would choose together. So, for their twentieth wedding anniversary in 1964, Dad bought Mum a platinum and white-gold eternity ring. It was simple but it suited her very slender fingers and I don't remember her ever taking it off. When she was dying, she wanted me to have it. But I couldn't bear to imagine Mum without it. Besides, it was even more of an emblem than a wedding ring – and I'd already got rid of one of those. So Mum was buried wearing her ring. And, although Mum knew how much I coveted her ruby ring, she insisted it should go to Frances – her first daughter's first baby girl. That's how important the symbolism of jewellery was to her, too.

But, after my first marriage ended, my lust for jewellery intensified. I was mesmerized by other women's flashy engagement and eternity rings. My ringless fingers were a constant humiliating reminder of my broken marriage – and a beacon sign to the world that I had failed. When I fell in love with Richard, I was giddy with joy when he presented me with a diamond gypsy-style ring to mark the anniversary of our first date. He extricated it carefully from his pocket over champagne at our favourite restaurant. Stunned by the gift, confused by its meaning, I asked him to put it on my hand. As he slipped it on the third finger of my right hand, I bit back my disappointment. But he guessed.

'This is for now. I'll buy you so many more rings in the future,' he promised. He knows his own mind. He won't be rushed, I thought, and I was even more convinced that this steady, feet-on-the-ground man was going to make my life complete. When he asked me to marry him a few months later, Richard suggested buying an engagement ring. But by then I loved that unassuming little ring so much, I refused. Like first love, it had meant so much that I couldn't bear to reject it.

And I wore it until the day my marriage ended. In fact, it was the moment when I ripped it off along with my wedding ring and hurled them both across the floor that I knew there was no going back. The tinkling sound as they collided with the wall was so pathetic that it made me want to weep even more.

And here I am, two years and three months later. I didn't have the faintest intention when I left home this morning of buying a ring for myself – ever. But as I admire the ring I'm thinking of buying, I realize with crystal-clear clarity that it isn't just covetable-gorgeous. It's life-affirming. Actually, not having a husband is irrelevant to how I feel about myself and how much love I have in my life. I don't need a man to buy me a ring to prove I'm worthy of love. And I'm damned if I can't buy my own ring and wear it on any finger I choose. In my eyes, *not* wearing it on my wedding ring would be a sign of defeatism. Wearing it says everything about how I feel at this moment and gives nothing away about my past or my future.

'Yes, I'll take it,' I say. The shop assistant is relieved. The girls are delighted. And I'm pleased that they are pleased for me. But I know the one person who will totally understand the significance of what I'm doing is Dad. He knows in a way I'm only beginning to appreciate that, to quote his beloved Shakespeare, 'Clothes maketh the man'. Or, in my case, 'A Dinny Hall ring maketh the woman'. And, sure enough, when we rush into his room with all our shopping bags to show him what we've bought in London, he smiles indulgently, delighted to see his girls so happy. He doesn't mention that it's pitch-black outside and, apart from his lunchtime visit, he's been alone all day. He wants to share in our pleasure.

'Wowee,' he whistles as he takes my hand so that he can examine the ring more closely. 'It's a dazzler all right.'

'But Dad, I'm afraid it was terribly expensive,' I confess, all little girl wanting reassurance.

Dad is totally nonplussed. 'Listen, Tetty. If it makes you feel good and look good, it's worth it,' he says, as I knew he would.

The truth is that, with every day, I'm learning more about how clothes are the best way Dad knows of maintaining his dignity.

I don't want to imply that Dad is – or has ever been – extravagant with clothes. Far from it. But he is acutely aware that if you look as though you care about your appearance, you'll exude confidence. My ever-dapper Dad may forget other things – whether it's lunchtime or teatime, whether it's five years or ten since his beloved big sister died – but, if I forget, which I sometimes do, to pop a freshly laundered hankie in his breast pocket, it's as though the sky has fallen in.

One of the most distressing things about visiting Dad in the care home was seeing him look unloved and uncared for. I'm not saying the staff didn't care or didn't do a good job. They did.

But they didn't know Dad the way I do. They didn't know that Dad likes to start every day on the off-chance that he might bump into the Queen: shoes buffed, trousers pressed, monogrammed handkerchief in breast pocket, jacket (blazer in the summer, sports jacket in the winter) immaculate – every spot of dirt brushed out, every piece of fluff picked off. Other dads may aspire to own Aston Martins or Harley-Davidsons, but for my dad, the acme of achievement was acquiring a Gieves & Hawkes sports jacket. Not surprising, I guess, when he'd spent his entire childhood in hand-me-downs.

Dad hates talking about his childhood. It stirs up memories he'd prefer to leave buried and reignites a sense of shame he has never quite lost. Although his father has been dead for over fifty years, Dad's resentment and contempt burn strong. Grandpa owned a small taxi business, one of the first in Newcastle, but he preferred to spend his days in the pub, drinking and cracking jokes with his mates, leaving Grandma with barely enough money to feed their ten children.

'I couldn't understand why the midwife kept coming to our house,' Dad muses. 'I'd see her marching down the street and pray she'd be going to another home – somewhere with fewer children. But no, it was always our house.'

Dad's biggest regret was that his future was sacrificed for a few coppers. A bright boy with a voracious thirst for knowledge, he wasn't allowed to go to St Cuthbert's, an academic secondary school, because his father wouldn't stump up to pay for the school uniform. Instead, Dad was dispatched to the local elementary Catholic school and to the mercies of a gang of poorly educated priests with a penchant for corporal punishment.

'There were boys who walked to school barefoot even in

the snow,' Dad says, and shudders. And I squirm with guilt, remembering the way I used to sneer whenever Dad mentioned St Cuthbert's because I thought it was such a stupid poncey name, not appreciating the trampled-on dreams it represented. He was nineteen before he had the money to buy his first suit – off the peg in a sale at Burton's 50 shilling tailor. Before then he'd lived in the same sports jacket and pair of flannels.

No wonder that, when he signed up with the RAF in 1936, he felt he'd been catapulted on to another planet.

'It was the first time in my life that I had my own bed,' Dad admits with a simplicity that takes my breath away. And as for the uniform – it made him feel like a rock star.

Mum's father disapproved of his treasured elder daughter marrying this Geordie Johnny-come-lately. But Dad, naturally the most respectful of men, found it hard to take him seriously. 'He was only a civilian,' he says. And the implication is obvious. Poor old Grandpa Connon may have thought quite well of himself as treasurer of the Royal Borough of Sutton Coldfield. But he wasn't an action hero like Dad. And, suddenly, I understand. Dad's RAF uniform didn't just confer instant sex appeal. It also commanded respect. As one of an elite band of heroes, a flight sergeant – later flight lieutenant – with the 85 Squadron, who'd saved the country from invasion during the Battle of Britain, he was virtually mobbed every time he left the base. And for Dad, the least vain of men, it was a stunning discovery.

It could all have gone to his head, but he was now a

married man and thinking of his family's future. He knew he'd need qualifications to get anywhere. So, in his spare time, he studied algebra, trigonometry and geometry – subjects he could barely spell, let alone understand. When the Education Act of 1944 introduced sweeping changes, including the introduction of the eleven-plus and an increased school-leaving age of fifteen, Dad realized there would be a need for more teachers. So, although he could have stayed in the RAF for another few years after the war, he jumped at the chance of a new career as a schoolmaster.

'It was a wonderful opportunity. They'd pay for me to train in twelve months rather than the normal two years and I would be set. It meant leaving Mum alone with little Hilary in Birmingham while I had to go up to Preston to train, but it was worth it.'

When Simon and Andy arrived, Dad got a job in Southend in Essex. He'd always loved the sea, and bounding down to the beach with a pile of sandwiches and a Thermos flask of tea was every bit as much of a treat for him as it was for my brothers and sister. It also meant that Dad could spoil the rest of the family, which really mattered to him. Every summer, cousins on both sides would bundle down for a seaside holiday and Dad would organize mass games of cricket on the sand. Brought up in the middle of Newcastle, he saw it as a children's paradise. But money was tight and when Dad's bike got a puncture and he couldn't even afford to buy a new tyre, he decided he'd had enough of scrimping and saving. So, in 1956, he took a pay rise to join the Army Education Corps, teaching young soldiers.

Dad made the most of being able to spend a bit of money on us. One of my earliest memories is of him taking me shopping. Being alone with Dad was strange enough. He wasn't the sort of hands-on dad who changed nappies or warmed up bottles. It was just before Easter. And what was so remarkable was that, without any discussion with Mum, Dad took me off into a ladies' clothes shop, where he personally selected a little straw hat with a jaunty yellow ribbon.

'You should have seen Mum's face when she saw you in your little Easter bonnet,' Dad chuckles. 'I don't think I've ever seen her look more surprised.'

And perhaps it's a particularly important memory, because actually I don't have very many memories of Dad during my childhood. This is perhaps the point at which to admit that while I was growing up – in fact, all the time my mother was alive – Dad and I weren't particularly close. I was a mummy's girl. I'm sure it wasn't what Mum intended, but she and I were such a double act that we shut him out. I was even called after Mum: Tessa to her Tess. And it's only now, as my own girls prepare to leave home, that I can see how it happened.

When I was four, Dad was posted to Germany. Fanatical about providing the very best education they could for us, it was then that my parents eagerly took up the offer from the army to pay for my sister and brothers to go to boarding school. For Dad, raised on *Magnet* comics with stories of

Billy Bunter and his boarding school for toffs, it seemed like a magic wand had been waved. His daughter would be a lady and his sons would be gentlemen.

Dad came back to England in 1966 while I was still at junior school. When he left the army a few months later, we settled near Southampton, so there was never any question of my going to boarding school. I was the last child, the only one at home, and, overnight, I became the focus of Mum's life. All through my teens I don't remember ever going out of my way to sit down for a conversation with Dad, whereas Mum and I would talk for hours on end.

And that's the way it stayed until Mum's death. Mum died just five months after I separated from my first husband. I was numb with shock – it had all been so quick – and suddenly I was faced with doing everything from pushing through a divorce to buying my own home, all without Mum's help. Instead, I leant on Dad hugely without a shadow of concern for what he was going through, and he didn't buckle. Not once, not a fraction.

When my first marriage ended and I decided to move out of London to Winchester, near where I grew up and where Dad still lived, he came house-hunting with me. And once I moved into my rather rackety 1950s house, it was Dad who organized workmen to do a whole host of renovations and gardeners to turn the quarter-acre of virtual wilderness into a manageable garden. He tried to do everything the man of the house should. On Mother's Day, he took the girls out to buy me primroses and showed them how to plant them. Although he was eighty, he taught them how to skip and chased them around the garden pretending to be the big bad wolf. And he did what he'd done for me. He bought them clothes. The girls were eight and six when Dad went to New York to stay with Simon. They drew pictures of the clothes they wanted him to bring back. He took the pictures around every conceivable shop – Macy's, Bloomingdale's, OshKosh – until he found the match. And when he opened his suit-case to show the girls, he was bursting with pride. As they paraded around in their co-ordinating sweatshirts and base-ball caps, he laughed.

'Don't they look bucked? The assistant said they'd look cute and they certainly do,' he said, and I could see he was relishing repeating a word he'd never used before.

True, Dad's forays into female shopping have always been rare, which makes them all the more precious. When we lived in Germany, Dad bought Hilary a beautifully styl-ish cape in cherry red. To save money, Mum normally made all her clothes. They were exquisitely tailored but they weren't always cutting-edge. This cape was different.

'She was pleased as punch.' He smiles. 'It was so smart. No one in England had anything like it. All her pals used to borrow it. I remember one day when we were driving through Oxford to her rooms, we saw her walking along the street. I stopped the car and beckoned her to get in. It was only then we realized that it wasn't Hilary at all. It was a pal. She'd borrowed Hilary's cape. When she married Brian and left

Oxford, her friends joked they'd miss her – but that they'd miss her cape even more.'

In later years, Dad would sneak off secretly and buy Mum a pair of gloves or a scarf for Christmas. They always came from her favourite store, Tyrrell & Green, part of John Lewis, and, in lieu of a receipt, Dad would write a little poem, all modest self-deprecation:

> My darling Tess, my dearest love,
> I had no one to guide me,
> Though I remember one fine day
> In Tyrrell's, you were beside me.
>
> I do recall, 'twas in the fall,
> When you did first descry it,
> This little thing did please you much,
> Though you were loath to buy it.
>
> Thus, my dear, with never a fear,
> I boldly said: 'By heck!'
> And bought this silken square in grey
> To grace your slender neck.
>
> So ends my tale and now, my love,
> To you with timid voice,
> I'll render up the bill of sale
> So you can make your choice.

Mum cried every single time. After she died, I found all the poems tucked away in her drawer where she kept her jewellery, her perfumes and – most precious of all – a little box of Elizabeth Arden soaps which was Hilary's last Christmas gift to her.

Unlike most of my friends' fathers, Dad was very indulgent of his girls and loved us to look good. He didn't understand female fashions – the very idea would have horrified him – but he understood perfectly why we wanted to look fashionable. And he didn't understand in the slightest why my brothers would not want to look smart. Dad seemed to spend my entire childhood in a state of permanent incomprehension that my brothers didn't share his exacting standards on gentlemanly attire. 'Put a razor across your face, lad,' he would sigh in impotent despair.

What possessed them to turn their noses up at Brylcreem, to grow their hair long, sport sideburns and wear Chelsea boots and denim jeans, when he could afford to buy them a sports jacket from Dunn & Co or Austin Reed? And when my nineteen-year-old cousin Michael came to join us for Christmas lunch in jeans and a duffel coat, Dad almost choked on his sherry. The addition of Michael's Oxford college scarf, flung carelessly over his turtleneck jumper, only intensified Dad's disgust.

'He's dressed like a scruffy beatnik, Tess. Can't his parents afford to buy him a decent suit? And what on earth do they say at Oxford?' he harrumphed at my mum.

When he lived alone, he kept religiously to Mum's pattern. Saturday was washing day. Monday was for ironing. He started taking over in the months before Mum died, even adding vacuuming and dusting to his list. And Dad didn't limit himself to ironing the absolute essentials. He'd stick the ironing board up in the living room and attack absolutely everything from hankies to underpants with great gusto.

He looked horrified when I asked him why he bothered. After all, no one would ever know if his boxers were crumpled or his vests creased. 'But I'd know.'

I had shuddered to see him in the care home. Sad, white bristles had sprouted from his chin and cheeks. The deep grooves around his mouth would often be stained with remnants of his lunch – tomato soup, chicken casserole, rhubarb and custard. His fingernails had been longer than I'd ever seen them. And, when I would bend to kiss him, his shirt collar smelled greasy where neither he nor his clothes had been washed properly.

One day I'd asked if Dad could, at least, get a proper shave every day. 'It depends who's on duty,' the manager had explained patiently. 'Not all the carers are trained in how to shave.'

Training in shaving? I had looked at her face and, honestly, she wasn't joking.

It had worried Dad – although, disorientated by his new life, he hadn't realized the extent of his deterioration. But it had worried me even more. I hated seeing my dad suddenly dishevelled and unkempt. He didn't seem like Dad any more. And God, did I know what that felt like. Losing my breast wasn't like losing an arm or a leg. It was like losing me.

*

When my breasts first started to grow, I was flooded with a mixture of fascination and fury. Though as tiny as oyster shells, they loomed as large as Blackpool Tower, flashing out in neon pink the message that my body was changing and there wasn't a thing I could do about it. If *Friends* had been on TV back in 1971, I'd have felt like Joey, who couldn't understand why women aren't playing with their breasts the whole time like he would. I was mesmerized by what was happening to my twelve-year-old chest. My head spun with questions: 'When can I get my first bra?' 'How big are they going to grow?' And then, for the next thirty years, I barely gave them a second thought, other than when yet another innocuous lump appeared. But now, in a bizarre rerun of history, faced with losing a breast, I found myself fixated on them all over again. I treasured them and loathed them with a sick, obsessive passion that was even more powerful than the first time around. I thought of little else, torturing myself with questions: What was happening inside them? How was I going to feel with just one breast? Lopsided? Freakish?

The day after I was told I was going to have to lose my breast, Richard and I had an appointment with the breast-care nurse, Sue. I was still in shock. Sitting in her airless little office, surrounded by leaflets on mastectomy swimwear and boxes of false breasts, it felt as though I'd been catapulted into a Monty Python sketch. The more she tried to make it seem normal, the more off the wall it seemed.

Sue was in full beauty-consultant mode. She must have thought it was reassuring. 'Would you like to look at some before-and-after photos to get an idea of what we can do for you?' she asked, pressing a photo album towards me.

I hadn't dared to imagine what to expect, but certainly it wouldn't have been this – an invitation to a grisly makeover courtesy of the NHS and a surgeon with a scalpel. How could I explain that examining photos of all the other poor souls who'd lain on that operating table before me would have been like rubbernecking at a car crash or watching a plane explode on the runway when you've just popped your boiled sweet into your mouth and are seconds from getting airborne?

Then, suddenly, a saying of Dad's jumped into my mind and I found myself almost smiling. When we were growing up, we used to take it in turns to trick Dad by giving him our breakfast boiled eggs, meat scooped out, shell turned upside down. Trying to keep a straight face, we'd pretend that we'd prepared a freshly boiled egg especially for him. Dad would play along with the joke time after time, hamming up his excitement at his wonderful yolky egg before rolling his eyes in disappointment. 'All right, you tinker. You've had your fun,' he would finally say in the mock-gruff voice he used just for this occasion.

But in the nurse's office, Sue was still doggedly running with the joke. On and on she went. 'There are so many wonderful things surgeons can do these days,' she said, smiling encouragingly.

I wanted to scream. 'Are you out of your mind? How

would you fancy having your breast sliced off and a false one slapped on? Keep your crazy makeovers, you lunatic.'

But I didn't. I simply stared straight ahead, gritted teeth hidden behind a false smile.

Finally, Richard stepped in. 'I think Tessa's made up her mind,' he said. 'We don't need to look at anything, thank you.' And, hand in hand, we stumbled out of there. I was shaking with the effort of trying to stop myself from dissolving on to the floor.

Outside, he hugged me. 'Don't think you have to do this for me,' he assured me. 'You'll always be the girlie I married.'

I truly believed he meant it, and his support helped to convince me. But I knew the most important thing to me was reclaiming my body. I would never feel the same about my breasts. How could I? But the thought of having a lookalike breast made out of flesh cut from my back with a nipple tattooed on sickened me. I would always look at it and feel revolted at this alien contraption mocking me for the real breast I had lost, the breast both lovely and diseased. It was like the day my aunty Kitty came to Ellen's birthday party in one of Mum's skirts. I loved her immensely. She was Dad's big sister and my favourite aunt, but that day I could cheerfully have ripped that skirt right off her. Mum had been dead two years and ever-generous Dad had believed that he was doing a good turn in offering out the remnants of her wardrobe. But seeing this woman who wasn't my mum in my mum's clothes opened the wound all over again.

I canvassed friends' opinion. Breasts. Women have them. But when we talk about them it's only to carp. Too big. Too small. Too droopy. Too saggy. Now I was about to have this most obvious demonstration of my femininity prised away from me. And I wanted to talk and talk and talk about what it would mean, how I would feel, because in all the time leading up to this moment, I had never actually believed that I would lose a breast. Now it was about to happen and I wasn't ready. Would I stop looking like a woman? Would I stop feeling like one?

Dyed-in-the-wool feminist Helen – always so cool and collected – stunned me: 'I'd definitely have a reconstruction. No question,' she said.

Madeleine, blonde and sexy, stunned me even more: 'If I had to lose a breast, I wouldn't give two hoots,' she said. 'In fact, I wouldn't mind losing them both. Honestly, they're just a pain in the neck.' That cheered me no end. It confirmed my deep-gut feeling – I didn't want a reconstruction.

I couldn't stop talking about breasts. But, most disconcertingly, I couldn't stop looking at them. Like some hormone-hijacked teenage boy, my eyes would wander unprompted to the chests of total strangers with a mixture of envy and fascination. Even when it came to meeting the surgeon the day before the operation, I found myself fixated on her bosom. She was plump but almost boyishly flat-chested, and I wondered what had possessed her to make her career in breast surgery. Did I trust her with mine? I had to, because, as she talked through my notes, I discovered just how bad things were.

'We found a lot more nasties when we did the last surgery,' she said. I went limp with fear. The cancer had learnt to mimic other cells – and had now spread to my lymph glands. Stupidly, I hadn't realized the implications – or hadn't wanted to. It wasn't just that the lymph glands had been breached and that the cancer cells were on the march, but they were using guerrilla tactics. They were embedding themselves in me, biding their time to kill me. That night – my last with my breast – I thought of asking Richard to photograph me. But I knew he'd find it macabre. Besides, I wasn't sure I could ever bear to look at the photo. Much better to try and forget I had ever been whole.

Coming around from the operation the next day, my face was wet with tears. It took me a while to realize that I wasn't crying because I was sad. It was relief. Back on the ward, which I shared with five others, breast cancer was the elephant in the room which we were all too polite to mention in case it set us off crying different tears – sad ones, frightened ones.

As the anaesthetic wore off, we munched biscuits, sipped tea and giggled about who'd got the sexiest hospital-regulation, tied-up-the-back nightgown. When a junior doctor arrived to check us over later that day, we could hear him through the curtains, prodding my poor flat-chested next-door neighbour. 'Just the one breast off, was it?' he asked.

'It was as though I'd diddled him out of a job,' she giggled later. We laughed as though it was the funniest thing we'd ever heard.

It meant that, for brief moments, I could pretend this was all perfectly normal and forget the one thing that dominated my thoughts – what my body looked like. I hadn't dared look at my breast. Every time the nurses came to check my wound, I squeezed my eyes shut. Into my head popped the newsreader's words before he or she announces the football score. 'If you don't want to know, look away now.' I repeated it like a mantra, struggling to recapture a world where anyone could care about football scores.

I still hadn't dared look when Richard arrived the morning after the operation to bring me home. It was a warm April day. The girls had gone off early to see Frances's baby Nancy christened. Ellen was her godmother. I should have been there too. Instead, Dominique, my oldest friend, had nobly offered to drive them there, promising to come back with every scrap of family gossip so I wouldn't feel as though I'd missed a thing. Now here I was in the garden, crying. I was lying on the sun lounger Richard had bought me in a bid to encourage the fantasy that I'd be enjoying the long days of summer soaking up the sun and not the reality that I was embarking on – months when all I'd be able to do would be to lie down, because moving would take too much effort. But I couldn't rest – not for a second. My exhausted brain was drawing increasingly hideous pictures. I saw a huge zig-zag wound. A caved-in chest. Blood oozing. I had to know the worst.

Richard came with me. I trusted him enough to believe that no matter what had been done, he wouldn't flinch. We stood side by side in front of the hall mirror. Gingerly, I unbuttoned my man's shirt. But I still didn't dare look. I listened for the faintest intake of breath, the slightest sign of shock from Richard.

But he was hugging me. 'It's fine, darling. It really is. You're still beautiful. You always will be. You brave, brave girlie,' and he kissed my cheek, now wet with tears. Only then did I dare open my eyes. My breast had vanished. In its place was a tiny pink line running from the middle of my chest to my armpit. It was almost dainty. One day, perhaps, I'd even be able to forget that there used to be a breast there. But not now. I cried huge, heaving sobs, grief-stricken at what I'd lost, and relieved that it was all over and that it wasn't worse, and I clung to Richard like a dog grips a bone. I needed his impassivity, his lack of imagination, his imperturbability. All the qualities that had begun to grate on me before I was ill, I now treasured. And all the other qualities – loyalty, bravery and a love for me that I didn't doubt for a second – seemed more valuable than ever. At that moment I think I honestly loved him more and felt closer to him even than I had the day we married.

Losing my breast was horrific. But it was just the beginning. When I'd recovered sufficiently from surgery I would start chemotherapy. The drugs would kill off all my body hair. What would be left of me then? I know some women loathe their hair, but, apart from the time when I was six and longed to look like Snow White so I, too, could live with the seven dwarves, I have always loved my long red hair. It was rare. It was prized. It was who I was. Long. Red. Hair. These were the first three words everyone used to describe me. My hair was the one thing everybody always commented on. It was the first thing Richard had fallen in love with. After a totally disastrous bob when I was fifteen and had had a sudden and woefully misguided urge to look like Mia Farrow in *The Great Gatsby*, my hair had never in thirty-three years strayed above my shoulders. I could not see a way of being me and not having my hair.

'What else are you going to take from me?' I raged at the cancer inside me.

And that's when I made one of the best decisions in this whole horrible, scary time. I decided to get a wig. Not any old wig. A wig that would mean no one would ever guess.

In one of her pep talks, Sue had explained that the NHS offers free wigs, but you are only allowed to choose from a limited price range.

'They're really very good these days,' she said. 'Honestly, you can never guess they aren't real.'

'Oh yeah,' I wanted to sneer. 'Maybe if you're a blind halfwit.' As you can tell – through absolutely no fault of her own – I was beginning to loathe this woman. She was the well-meaning messenger who always brought me bad news. What I'd get would be an acrylic wig in a colour and style that might approximate to mine but definitely wouldn't allow me to feel like me. And that's what I needed right now.

Having only one breast made me feel self-conscious enough. But I was damned if I was going to look like a freak in a wig. I'd seen enough cancer patients in perky headscarfs and ill-fitting wigs to know that I absolutely, one hundred per cent couldn't bear to look like that, to feel strangers' eyes slide away from mine with a mixture of pity and embarrassment. The second I decided to take action, I felt better.

Long ago, in a different life, I interviewed Richard Mawbey, wig-maker to the stars. The interview was about his work on *Star Wars* – he was responsible for Ewan McGregor's weird Obi-Wan Kenobi look. But our conversation had touched on other celebrities. He had created a wig for Linda McCartney, making her look terrific after she had lost all her blond hair to breast cancer. She hadn't simply still looked beautiful – she had looked like herself. I thought a lot about Linda McCartney, although I tried not to. I much preferred to think about Kylie Minogue, Olivia Newton John, Marsha Hunt and Sheryl Crow. In fact, anyone who had ever had breast cancer and had survived. It's like when you have a baby and for those first few months you are convinced you are united in a soppy, milk-soaked communion with every other woman on earth who's ever done this extraordinarily brutal, brave and unbelievable thing of giving birth. A sort of worldwide group hug of sleep-deprived, weepy, over-sensitive new mums. Now I felt the same visceral bond with all the women who'd had breast cancer before me. Battle-scarred survivors, they pointed the way for me, allowing me to believe that I, too, might – just might – get through this.

I dug out my old notebook from 1999 and Googled Richard Mawbey. His site is a roll-call of starry clients – Sean Connery, Susan Sarandon, Burt Reynolds, Madonna, Kylie Minogue, Kate Beckinsale. And then I saw the price – £1,650.

Ordinarily, that would have put me off there and then. I'm such an inveterate bargain hunter that I bought my first wedding dress in a sample sale and my second off the peg at Monsoon for under £100. But it didn't. In fact, it made me even more enthusiastic. I was in a mood to be totally, wildly self-indulgent. When I told Richard, he was supportive, but I could tell he didn't understand.

'It's a lot of money. Don't feel you have to do it for me – honestly, you don't,' he said, totally missing the point.

It was Dad who had really encouraged me. He'd under-stood instinctively how badly I needed to look like me, even if it was make-believe. 'Whatever it costs, you do it,' he said. 'If you really want it, get it. And if you need money, you know you only have to ask. What else am I going to spend my money on? Gambling? Round the world cruises?' Merci-fully, I didn't need Dad's money, but his instant generosity warmed me. He knew the wig wasn't a foolish indulgence. It was sticking two fingers up at cancer. It was proclaiming to the world: 'I'm worth it.' It was making choices. It was taking control. And, most important of all, it was ensuring that no one would guess that I was ill, no one would dare pity me or patronize me. Because the one thing I couldn't bear was for anyone to feel sorry for me.

My old *Sun* friend Madeleine came with me for my consultation. Up the creaky stairs of the anonymous-looking building off Marylebone Road we teetered, goggling at all the film and stage posters on the walls, and there was Richard, all luxuriant silver-grey hair and neatly trimmed moustache. He claimed to remember me, but I felt like a pathetic shadow of the national-newspaper feature writer who had swanned into his office in my other life – cherry-red leather briefcase under my arm, high heels, tight black Jigsaw skirt and cream silk blouse. However, Richard was adept at appearing completely unfazed. Over mugs of tea, he measured my head to get a perfect fit, took photos and snippets of my hair so that he could get the right match, and all the while we gossiped. And when Madeleine and I finally left, I didn't feel scared. I actually felt excited. I was so eager to try my new look that I honestly felt I could lose all my hair without batting one of my (about to be) lash-free eyelids.

And God, did I need that confidence, when, three weeks after my first chemo, my hair started coming out in handfuls. I was like a Christmas tree left out for the bin men. Hanks of hair dropped off me like drifts of pine needles. Great wodges stuck to my brush, and when I had a bath hair pooled around me like road kill, manky and lifeless. Lying in the bath, clumps of hair clinging to my scarred body like seaweed, I honestly thought of drowning myself. I felt so desperate, so utterly, completely hopeless. Did it really matter whether I lived or died when the me that was me had already gone?

At home, Richard said something that made me want to live – just so that I could kill him.

'Shall I run the vacuum cleaner over your head?' he asked, bending to pick up a handful of loose hair from the bedroom floor. I knew he was joking and trying to lighten the mood, but because of the circumstances it didn't work. I felt as though I had shifted – so imperceptibly that I'd barely noticed – from being his feisty wife, brimming with self-confidence and health, to becoming an object.

Ellen was in the room. 'Men are so stupid sometimes, Mummy,' she said, rushing to hug me.

Richard looked shamefaced. 'Darling, you know I didn't mean to upset you. I was just joking. It was stupid. I'm sorry.' But I was stunned. How could my loving, supportive husband, who I thought was closer to me than anyone else on earth, be so unfeeling?

Only the prospect of my wig sustained me. It would be ready in a week. But I had to take action – now. I rang Eleanor, my lovely beautician. 'I'm begging a favour,' I explained.

'Anything,' she said, and I started crying as I explained what was happening. I cried even more when Richard drove me over to her house. She opened her door and gave me a huge hug. Richard suggested shaving my head. Eleanor brushed him aside. 'We haven't got to that stage,' she said. 'We can do a really nice close crop.' She did. I actually looked presentable – in a menopausal punk sort of way. It was a new me. Not ugly, not terrifying. Just different. Most of all I didn't want to scare the girls. I promised Elise she would never have to see me bald. She was the child who cried the first time she ever saw me in a shower cap.

That's why I asked her to come with me to collect the wig. I sold it to her as an exciting day out in London to meet the man who rubbed shoulders with Ewan McGregor, and hoped it would ease her fear of seeing me go bald.

We were thirty minutes early for the appointment, so we walked around the streets. We found ourselves outside the flat in Crawford Street where my friends Helen and Peter and then Bridget had lived after Oxford – I'd no idea it was so near. Standing outside the blue front door felt like a good omen. I texted Peter and told him where I was and what I was doing. 'Good luck,' he texted back.

And then I was trying the wig on. And, in the time it took to adjust it and look in the mirror, I was me again. The colour was mine. The style was me, fresh out of the hair-dresser's – red hair tumbling in waves to my shoulders. I looked over at the wall and there was a photo of Susan Sarandon on the red carpet in her Richard Mawbey wig. We looked like we'd just stepped out of the same hairdressers. In the mirror I could see Elise's face behind me. Her eyes were all misty like mine. I made her take notes about all the care instructions – to do with sticky tape and washing. I was too excited to concentrate. I'd slunk into the salon in my ludicrous headscarf. I walked out, sassy and glamorous. The taxi driver smiled at me. And I realized it was the first time I'd had the confidence to look a stranger – particularly a man – in the face since this whole wretched business started. Peter sent me a text: 'Are you bewigged, bothered and be-wildered?' Not likely. 'I'm bewigged, beautiful and blos-soming,' I texted back. On the train home I couldn't stop playing with my hair. It was soft, luxuriant and so, so real.

Dad never commented on my new hair and it was exactly what I needed – he was making it clear that I looked like me and it helped me to feel like me. By following Dad's example and facing life – and cancer – looking and feeling the best I could, I had the strength and confidence to get through my treatment. It might sound trivial but, when I was at my absolute lowest, I always had the comfort of my beautiful head of hair. And when it was over, my own hair grew back, emerging first tentatively and then abundantly from beneath my Richard Mawbey locks.

The day I finally cast off the wig, Dad looked me up and down and said, 'Your hair looks lovely today, Tetty. Have you done something different with it?' I don't think he quite understood why I laughed, and then rushed to hug him. The funniest thing of all was that I discovered short hair actually suits me much better than long hair had. I've never grown it long again. And if I hadn't lost my hair, I'd never have known.

FIVE

ONE STEP AT A TIME

Dad took my illness completely in his stride. So much so, in fact, that there were times when his equanimity drove me mad. He pretended my cancer wasn't happening. As far as he was concerned, I had nothing more life-threatening than a common cold. And that was the story he stuck to. Although he'd so generously offered to pay for my wig, he proceeded to completely ignore my hair falling out. He didn't ask what had happened at my chemo sessions – managing to convince himself that the cancer was simply an unsightly lump under my arm which had been successfully removed.

Apart from when Mum died, Dad has absolutely no personal experience of serious illness, which leaves him woefully lacking in sympathy. Even now he never gets colds, and, apart from the paracetamol which I press on him in the hope it might ease the discomfort of his arthritis, he has no conception of being in pain. He spent my entire childhood yearning to be ill just so that Mum would fuss over him.

But he's got the constitution of an ox. And when finally he did become ill in 1984, it was with a heart attack. Poor Dad. Instead of the longed-for treats that invalids normally get, Mum instituted a strict regime and a low-fat diet. No more puddings. No more custard. Cheese board only once a week. Low-fat spread instead of butter.

Mum bought a steamer and served endless amounts of healthy steamed cabbage and broccoli. She made her own muesli and flapjacks, baked wholemeal brown loaves and developed a passion for grains and nuts. Totally against his will, Dad, in his seventies, found himself being turned into a health-food junkie. His only treat was sirloin steak on his birthday. But it can't have been much of a pleasure as poor Mum managed unfailingly to cremate it.

The ironic thing was that I'd actually psyched myself up to tell him about my cancer, worried that he was going to fall apart. I was aware enough of his feelings and his need to protect his little girl to understand that it would be painful learning that I was seriously ill.

So I tried to put the most positive spin on it that I could as I broke the news to him – just the two of us, over a cup of tea in his flat.

'Daddy, I don't know how to say this any other way, but I've got breast cancer. I didn't want to tell you earlier, because I didn't want you to worry. I've had an operation and the lump's gone. But I've got to have chemotherapy over the summer. You know what that is, don't you?'

Dad nodded. I could see he was visibly shaken. And

that's when – despite my best intentions – I went to pieces. As I sobbed, Dad hugged me and stroked my hair.

'There, there, sweet. It will be all right. Mum will look after you, I know she will,' he said.

And then he gave me some of the best advice. I just wish I'd understood it at the time. 'Just deal with what you can and leave the rest for another time.'

And after that he carried on as normal – following his own advice to the letter, as he still does today. Dad pretended that nothing extraordinary was happening, nothing that we couldn't cope with.

I'm certain that Dad sees the absurdity in his condition, the fact that he's beginning to need help doing even the simplest of physical things. He doesn't rail against it and refuses to worry about what might be around the corner. Logically, he must know that his arthritis is going to get worse, that there might come a time when he's too weak even to walk from his bed to his armchair. But, if he thinks about it at all, he certainly doesn't mention it.

However, in those first few months when he refused to acknowledge my cancer, it drove me wild with fury and frustration. I could not understand why he would choose to ignore the blindingly obvious. I thought it was cowardly and I was really angry. I didn't understand that, in fact, knowing how much you can cope with and refusing to acknowledge problems you know you can't deal with takes a lot of self-knowledge and wisdom.

I was too bound up in my own problems to understand

that Dad knew that the only way he could be strong for me was to stay positive and stoic himself. He saw his job as being there for me to lean on through thick and thin. That meant refusing to allow his imagination to run riot.

He'd been exactly the same when my mother was dying. When Mum was diagnosed, it was too late for anything more than palliative treatment. She was taken to hospital on Christmas Day and never came home, dying on 3 January 1995. In the last few months, she did everything conceivable to prove that she knew her condition was terminal. She organized the family photo album; she completed all her sewing projects; she insisted on giving Dad a crash course in cookery. She even took Dad to the local cemetery and pointed out where she would like to be buried. Given her passion for gardening, its position next to a potting shed couldn't have been better appointed.

But Mum never said the words 'I am dying'. Not to me, not to anyone. What she told me was that she had asked the consultant whether she would be alive to see the blossoming of the spring bulbs that she had planted.

'Let's hope so,' he had told her. She was such a rational woman, I'm sure she couldn't possibly have believed those words were a glowing testimonial on the state of her health. But if she was frightened, she never let on. And while I can see now that both she and Dad were fully aware of the reality, Dad maintained right until the bitter end that she was going to get better.

When she died early that January morning, Dad and I

were at her bedside. As we kissed her for the last time and walked out of that bleak, windowless hospital room, I expected him to fall apart.

But he didn't. In fact, it was Dad who supported me. 'She's in a much better place now, love. You know that, don't you?' he said, as he hugged me. And I realized then that what I had taken for wilful naïvete was actually a means of protecting himself and Mum. They must have made a pact not to mar their last precious months together with talk of death. What was the point, when they had said everything they needed to in the fifty years they had been married?

Perhaps this attitude was acquired during the Battle of Britain. On the first day, Dad's commanding officer called all the men together. 'This will possibly be the last time you will all meet as, sooner or later, some of you won't come back from missions,' he explained. He drummed it into his men never to dwell on the missions they'd been on – or the missions they faced. It was a way of acknowledging the truth but refusing to let it affect their performance.

'Leave it in the hangar,' became Dad's refrain. He knew never to talk shop and that the best way to cope with fear is simply to 'get stuck in', as he would put it. And that seems to be what he has been doing ever since – with gusto.

As I may have mentioned before, Dad has arthritis. When he moves, his knee joints creak so loudly you'd swear someone was cracking nuts. When he walks, he's in pain. And standing for more than a few minutes is a perilous business because there's always the danger that his knees will give way altogether. As everyone with arthritis knows, it's a progressive condition which can only get worse. Dad knows this, too – the doctor has explained it to him often enough. The conversations go something like this:

Dad: 'I can't play golf or go dancing any more because my knees hurt. Is there anything you can do, doctor?'

Doctor: 'I'm afraid not, Mr Cunningham. You've got arthritis and I can't give you new knees.'

Dad: 'How about an oil can, then, to lubricate the joints?'

Doctor: 'I'm afraid that's not been invented yet, Mr Cunningham. But when it has, you'll be the first to know.'

Dad doesn't ask for a detailed prognosis or worry about what the future holds. He lives in the moment, secure in his own little bubble. It's his way of dealing with what he can cope with at the time and not allowing himself to worry about what may or may not be in store.

And now I discovered, how deep that lesson had penetrated, because I found myself doing exactly the same. When I lost my breast, I hadn't dared imagine what would happen next. It was a step too far. But as I prepared to start my chemotherapy treatment, it was time to face up to what had happened. It was time to pick up my prosthesis – another step along this perilous, uncharted path that I couldn't face thinking about because it made the whole situation so horrifically real. It was one thing losing a breast; it was quite another being measured up for a synthetic replacement 'breast form'. I felt sick with humiliation and angry, angry,

angry with all the other women in the world walking around with a full complement of breasts.

It was 1 June and I went to the hospital alone, as Richard was working and this was one job I felt I should be brave enough to handle by myself. I hadn't dared look at any pictures on the Internet. I hadn't dared contemplate what to expect. But, as Sue ushered me into her office and took the prosthesis out of the box, I knew this wasn't it – this pinkish lump of sploshy silicone that looked like a jellyfish and felt like a slab of smoked salmon. I wanted my lovely real breast back, with the real blood flowing through it, the real skin and the real nipple. Her words washed over me as I dug my nails in my hand and tried not to cry. I didn't want to hear about something called 'free pocketing' done on the NHS. I didn't want to think of handing in my lovely La Perla and Freya bras and having them come back as surgical appliances with hideous pockets sewn in to hold my hideous prosthesis – and reeking of bleach and boiled cabbage.

Seeing the look of undisguised horror on my face, Sue dived into her drawer and came out brandishing a huge rubber breast.

'Look, it's not for ever. You could graduate to this when the scarring has totally healed,' she said.

Apparently this Kenny Everett-style monstrosity was a stick-on breast. I couldn't even bear to go down the road of asking what it sticks on with. Pritt Stick? Sellotape? A staple gun? I was so angry I just wanted to stick it down her throat and run.

But I couldn't. Sue urged me to 'pop' my prosthesis between my naked chest and my bra to check it was the right size. Personally, I'd gone beyond caring. One breast could be borrowed from Katie Price, for all I was bothered. However, as the prosthesis threatened to slither down my chest and straight out of my T-shirt, it was obvious that this could only be a temporary solution. And, as I'd rather have chucked all my lingerie away than hand it over to the NHS to be 'pocketed', I listened, dazed, as Sue explained that I'd need to buy special 'post-operative bras'.

'You can buy them from specialist shops or even Marks and Spencer,' she said encouragingly.

And that's how Richard and I found ourselves wandering around the lingerie department of Marks and Spencer in Blackwater, Berkshire. We had driven Dad to Wokingham, where he was spending the weekend with Frances, her partner Paul and their daughter Nancy, and we were on our way home when I suggested we stop off. I had done my research and knew this branch sold specialist bras. Ever since I'd had the mastectomy, I'd steeled myself against looking at bras. I'd deliberately taken long and convoluted detours in department stores to avoid even the remotest chance of finding myself in a lingerie section. I'd averted my eyes whenever lingerie adverts came on the TV, and when I accidentally found myself tuning in to a Trinny and Susannah special on underwear, I had to run from the room before the girls could see me cry. Now, as the tears sprang to my eyes, I realized I couldn't protect myself from the truth for ever. It was unbearably painful. There were rows and rows of flimsy, silky, lacy bras in beautiful colours and styles – balconette, padded, push-up and plunge – and I would never be able to wear any of them ever again. I was stumbling around, sniffing and sobbing, trying to find the section for misshapen women and hoping that no one would notice I was distressed or – horror of horrors – ask what I was looking for. Because if they did, I'd start crying properly and then I wouldn't be able to stop.

Richard had got his strong, determined look on – eyes slightly moist, jaw clenched – as he put his arm around my shoulder and steered me towards the section bluntly labelled 'Post Operative'. I didn't want to linger. I barely wanted to look. But, luckily, there wasn't exactly an overwhelming choice. There were just five styles and they all looked as though they'd been designed to appeal to a well-upholstered matron who'd sworn off sex for the last twenty years. I grabbed a couple of the least middle-aged styles I could find in my size and slunk off to the changing room before I could catch anyone's eye. Was this what it felt like to have to buy incontinence pads, or those helpful kits for perimenopausal women, telling them how long it would be before they were completely barren? This same heavy, hot weight of intense embarrassment and shame?

I didn't want to spend a second longer than I needed in the changing room. I didn't even want to look at myself, but, mercifully, one of the styles – a simple T-shirt-style bra with a special pocket for my prosthesis – fitted. I found another in my size and, with Richard behind me, walked over to the bank of tills, trying to look as though this was just a normal purchase on a normal day. But the assistant had other ideas. Holding the bras aloft, she looked me quizzically up and down. 'You do realize these are post-surgery?' she said in a voice the entire queue could hear.

I shot her a look of utter hatred and nodded my head mutely. 'Then you've got to fill in a form,' she said, rummaging in a folder beside the till.

A form? Did Marks and Spencer keep a list of all its one-breasted customers? Would I need to prove it? Just how much worse could this get?

By now, the customers behind me were getting restless. But Richard was at my side. 'It's all right, darling. You just need to sign a form because there's no VAT on these sorts of bras,' he whispered. He took the pen from the assistant and filled in my name and address before gently getting me to sign.

I stumbled outside. Suddenly I realized why there was no VAT on my bras – because they were classed as disability aids. I was now officially a disabled person. I was crying now, and Richard did the only thing he could think of to take my mind off what had happened. He steered me along the shopping mall and into Tesco, which was right next door. He was taking Elise windsurfing the following day with one of his clients, a widow in her early sixties called Karen Taylor, and wanted to buy a picnic lunch for them all.

*

Over the years, Karen had become one of Richard's best clients. She had a smart four-bedroom detached house in a pleasant road on the outskirts of Winchester, with a large garden. I'd clocked it eagerly when I walked up the drive to drop one of Richard's flyers through her letterbox one day back in April 2003, when I was trying to help him kick-start his business.

I didn't meet Karen – I rarely met any of Richard's clients, although I heard a lot about them – but, from what he told me over the years, I had built up a picture of a wealthy, independent-minded but very lonely woman. I felt sorry for her. In fact, it was because of her lonely state that I first became conscious of Karen. Richard had been working for her for about a year. We were all having supper and Richard was talking about what he had been up to that day.

'I was helping Karen with her garden this morning and she got upset all of a sudden. Something to do with her family, I think. I ended up having to comfort her. I gave her a hug. I didn't know what else I could do,' Richard said.

I didn't know what he could have done, either. So I said: 'Of course you did the right thing, darling. But be careful she doesn't come to rely on you too much.' And I felt quietly smug that I was married to the sort of nice, kind man who would go out of his way to be helpful.

Karen was keen on windsurfing and seemed to travel constantly, pursuing her hobby. Richard talked about all his clients and, because I'm so nosey, I loved to hear the minutiae of what was going on. There was Sue with the outdoor pool,

Sarah with the sit-on lawnmower, Phil with the wine cellar, Chris with the summer house, Lucy with the dogs, and, of course, Karen. I heard all about the new sandstone terrace Karen had had laid. Richard was so impressed that, when we came to build a new terrace, he suggested buying the very same tiles. I heard all about how she preferred Tesco to Sainsbury's and rated the Tesco fresh fish counter the best in Winchester. I heard all about her property in the Caribbean, which was apparently proving a bit of a millstone. It needed constant maintenance and, although Karen employed a local handyman, he hadn't proved particularly reliable.

Richard had been working for her for about two years when she asked if he'd be prepared to go over to the Caribbean. He would work for free, but she would pay his airfare and, in return, we could have a family holiday in the apartment whenever it suited us. He'd only be gone for a week. It was January. It was bitterly cold and even his regular clients didn't need him. It all made perfect sense. He'd be enjoying the sunshine and cementing a good relationship with a valued client.

'I won't go if you need me here,' he said when, tentatively, he made the suggestion. 'You and the girls come first.'

He showed me Karen's property on the Internet. Built on a former sugar plantation, it had a website devoted to its amenities: the en suite bathrooms; the stunning views of the Atlantic Ocean; the infinity pool; the island's premier golf course next door; the maid service; the walk-in shower; the huge American Maytag fridge-freezer and ice-maker. It was jaw-droppingly impressive and I knew I'd feel mean saying no. I asked if Karen would be staying there, too, but that wasn't the case, apparently. It seemed like a good work opportunity, so I happily agreed to Richard going.

Once there, he rang and texted every day with a mixture of how difficult it was to galvanize the local workmen into action and how beautiful and lush everything was. Back home in dreary Winchester, I felt a mixture of envy and delight. And I wasn't a bit surprised when he came back, a week later, on a high. 'I can't wait to take you there. Karen's house is just amazing and the beaches and the wildlife are out of this world,' he said. 'The girls would flip over the pool.'

Sadly, our promised family holiday never materialized. The ideal time to go would be Christmas, when the British weather is at its worst and the weather in the Caribbean at its best. But of course that's when the cost of flights rocket.

And then I became ill. Holidays were out of the question. Richard could not do enough to care for me. And the more attentive and solicitous he was, the more I came to rely on him. It was a huge turn-around from just a few months previously, when I had been fit and healthy and, in so many ways, the one calling the shots. It was such a big responsibility and Richard took it all so seriously that I was beginning to worry it was too much. I could be on the phone from morning till night chatting to various friends, but Richard had no one to chat to, no one to offload on to. He had close friends in London, but as to whether he actually confided in them, I had no idea.

After all, picking over the minutiae of life is not what most men do, certainly not in my experience. My dad may be far more convivial than Richard, but he was never what you would call clubbable. Or, at least, not until Mum died. While Mum was alive, Dad resisted joining any group or committing himself to any regular activity that would oblige him to turn up at a particular time on a particular day. He said he wanted to be able to put his family first, but I think it probably had more to do with kicking over the traces of his life in the services, where his freedom was curtailed. When Mum retired, she joined a weekly sewing class and became a co-worker of Mother Teresa, part of a band of women from the local Catholic church who met weekly to pray and raise money to help the famous orphanage in Calcutta. Dad followed happily in her wake. Together they visited an elderly spinster, Nellie Nagel. They became incredibly fond of her. While Mum sat and chatted with her, Dad would pace around the flat until he found something practical to do, such as cleaning out her fridge or returning her library books. They carried on visiting her until the day she died.

I was very worried that, when Mum died, Dad wouldn't be able to fill his days. He had tons of acquaintances, but he'd made all his friends through Mum. And most of them were couples. In their company, poor Dad felt like an encumbrance. So I was both stunned and delighted when he forged out by himself and joined the local Conservative Club, purely because he had been told that they had a snooker table. And of course it was there that he discovered tea-dancing. Dad was in his element, waltzing around the floor with a bevy of women a good ten or twenty years younger than him. In fact, no one would ever have guessed his age if I hadn't written a story for the *Daily Mail* about my eighty-six-year-old father's new hobby.

His new friends were stunned. 'Eighty-six, Jim? You never are. We thought you were only seventy,' they clucked. Dad liked to blame me for ruining any burgeoning romance with this revelation. But the truth is that he talked so much about Mum and his family that it was perfectly obvious he wasn't remotely interested in a new relationship. He just enjoyed the banter. I was really pleased when, long after I was better, Dad told me that he had talked over my illness with his favourite dance partner, Beryl.

'It's great that you were able to share, Dad.'

Dad looked flummoxed. 'Share?' he repeated, as though I'd suggested some outlandish practice.

'Never mind – it's just a way of saying you're lucky to have a lovely friend you can talk to.'

Dad's face cleared. 'I certainly am. I know I'm a silly old fool, but she's very patient with me.'

I was convinced that Richard needed an outlet, so I was pleased when he asked tentatively one day in late May if I'd mind him spending a couple of hours windsurfing with Karen. I knew how much Richard loved the sea. Being by the sea, even for a day, would be a welcome distraction for him, away from my sickbed and the grind of caring for me. I was insistent that he go. All I cared about was preserving enough strength to see me through the months of treatment on the horizon.

He came home happy and energised, his eyes shining with the fun of it all. So, when he asked to go on several more windsurfing trips with Karen, I was fine about it. He even took Elise one time. I was delighted to see him happy, not just for his sake but for mine – I was relying on him increasingly to keep my spirits up, too.

Sometimes when he was away, I was nervous and frightened of being alone with my thoughts, but, even so, I didn't ask him to stay behind. That would have meant admitting my terror of cancer to myself, and I was too frightened of the demons I might unleash to risk doing that. The days before my chemotherapy sessions were the worst. When he wasn't around, I became more anxious – and it was then that I started to become suspicious.

One afternoon, Richard was out windsurfing when I found myself overcome with dread. I tried reading. I tried watching TV. But nothing could lift my mood. As the hours ticked by, I found myself pacing around the house, desperate for Richard to hug me and tell me everything would be all right. When the phone rang and it was Richard, relief flooded through me – it meant he would be back soon – but he said something about being stuck in terrible traffic and told me he'd be late.

Was it my heightened sensibilities that made me think something wasn't right? I don't know. But he sounded odd to me and for some reason my trust in him was shaken. Honesty is so deeply ingrained in me, I'll even ruin a perfectly good story just to get the punch line entirely accurate. It's inconvenient; it's a curse. And it's also a blind spot because it means I always assume other people are telling the truth, too.

I got it from Mum. As far as she was concerned, lying wasn't just morally wrong. It was intellectually stupid, which was almost as bad.

'Lying is destructive,' she always said. 'It hurts you and it also hurts everyone around you. People lie about something when they are ashamed. And you should never do anything you are ashamed of because, in the end, it will just make you unhappy.'

Of course she fibbed socially – very occasionally and to avoid wounding people's feelings. But it was always with such an effort, the look of grim concentration on her face was almost laughable.

'Mum, do you really like this piece of naff artwork knocked up at school/hideous pair of tights in American Tan/nylon nightie that's two sizes too small/book you've read already?' we'd ask.

'Um, yes, very nice,' she would fib gamely – and totally unconvincingly.

The thought of my parents lying to one another is inconceivable, even though I know Dad is capable of bending the truth on occasion. When he was offered promotion in the RAF, one of the prerequisites was that he came from a service background 'Oh, yes, sir. My father was in the Northumberland Fusiliers in the First World War,' he replied quickly – knowing full well his that father had been a draft dodger. Although I can't imagine my parents ever lying to each other, there are definitely things Dad avoided telling Mum because he knew that she would disapprove. When my parents decided to move from Sutton Coldfield to Southend, Mum went house-hunting. She found the perfect home – a three-bedroom detached house with a huge garden near the sea. There was only one catch: it had gone under offer that very day.

Dad was having none of it. If Mum wanted the house then he would do his damnedest to get it for her. He went charging off to the estate agent's the next morning.

'I need your help. My wife has fallen in love with one of your houses and I can't disappoint her.'

Patiently, the agent explained the situation.

'But they haven't actually put any money down yet, have they?' said Dad, seizing his opportunity. 'How about I go for lunch, and when I come back I'd like to see all the paperwork done – and here's something for you to have a nice meal with your wife?'

Dad handed over a crisp £5 note – the equivalent of £50 today. Sure enough, when he came back from lunch the house was his. But he never told Mum how he had clinched the deal. She would have hit the roof.

There are people who fib glibly to extract themselves from awkward situations or to make life easier for themselves and their loved ones, but Richard wasn't one of them. His honesty was one of the qualities I really admired in him. Even when he'd forgotten to phone his mum, to pick up some dry-cleaning or to video *Desperate Housewives* for me, Richard was scrupulously truthful. I told myself I must be imagining things. But I knew from his slightly excitable tone during that brief phone call that I wasn't. He was lying – and it was a horrible, mean, insulting lie – the sort you tell your boss when you're late for work and can't think of a good enough excuse. It wasn't the sort of lie you tell to a wife you're supposed to love and respect. A sixth sense told me to look in the cupboard where we kept the wine. A bottle of expensive rioja was missing. Wine that Richard had bought on Karen Taylor's recommendation.

I needed to know the truth. I hadn't driven since the operation. But I got in the car and I drove to her house. I didn't even know the exact address, but I remembered the road from the time when I'd posted one of Richard's flyers through the letter box. I cruised along the road, hoping against hope that I was wrong. But no. There, in the drive of one of the houses, was Richard's car. I wanted to run up the drive, hammer down the door and confront him, but I was scared of what I was about to unleash and where it could lead.

So I didn't. I went back home and I waited for Richard's return. Less than thirty minutes later, I heard his car pull up and I walked slowly out to meet him. He was already unloading his kit from the boot. He looked up, he looked me in the eyes, and he started lying – again.

'I left on time but it was bumper to bumper. I'm so sorry. Let me freshen up and I'll start getting supper ready.'

Panic was mounting. I could feel my chest tighten. I felt sick.

'You're lying,' I said and my voice was a strangled whisper. 'I saw your car at Karen Taylor's. You weren't stuck in traffic. You were at her house.'

Richard's face clouded over with shame and embarrassment.

'Oh darling, I'm so sorry,' he said, and he rushed to hug me. 'It was wrong of me to be there, wrong of me to lie to you. We got back from windsurfing early because the tides weren't right. Karen offered to help me practise putting up sails in her garden. We did that for about an hour and then she offered me a drink. I know I should have said no and come straight home. But I've been so worried about you and all you've been going through and I just needed time out.'

'But you took a bottle of wine?'

'It was just a little present to say thank you for her lending me her husband's old surfboard.'

'Is that all? Then why did you lie to me?'

'I felt guilty. I should have come straight home, and when I realized the time, I felt so bad I couldn't bear to tell you the truth. I'm sorry.'

Mum, 'the reluctant bride', and Dad on their wedding day in 1944.

Above Dad, Andy, aged ten, and me, aged two.

Left My parents as a young married couple, outside their first home in Sutton Coldfield.

On the beach with Dad and my brothers.

Southsea beach on a chilly day with our dog Sammy.

Above Dad taking me swimming at a local lido, aged six.

Right A bedtime story.

Below With Dad in a rowboat on holiday in Holland.

Hilary, off to boarding school, with Dad, 1961.

The whole family: Mum, Hilary, me, Simon, Andy and
Dad in the garden of our home in Germany, 1964.

Above Hilary on her graduation day with me and a very proud Dad.

Right Mum and Dad with Ellen.

Below At Ellen's second birthday party with Mum and Elise.

Mum and Dad celebrating their fiftieth wedding anniversary at home.

Mum and Dad with the girls.

With Ellen, aged four, and Elise, aged two.

Dad, adjusting his hearing aids, at my fiftieth birthday party.

Our family: Dad, the girls and me.

With Dad in his favourite spot in our garden.

'Are you honestly telling me that there is nothing going on between you?'

Richard looked shocked. 'Of course not,' he said. 'How can you even imagine anything so daft? She's lonely and she's trying to be kind – that's all. What I did was really selfish. And it was stupid of me to lie to you. It was only because I felt so bad. It won't happen again, I promise.'

And as I cried and buried my head in his chest, I believed him. Anything else was unthinkable. I was sick. I was frightened. I had months of treatment ahead of me. To get through it I had to stay focused. I had to take life one step at a time, just like Dad had always done. I needed a husband I could trust implicitly. So I trusted him. I had to.

SIX

CHOOSE YOUR MEMORIES

Watching Dad creep across the room in his carpet slippers, back stooped, wincing at every move, it is almost impossible to imagine that only a few years ago he would stride the twenty minutes into town, arms behind his back as though he were still on the parade ground. He would play golf in the morning, race home in his little white Peugeot for a shower and a bowl of soup, and then charge out again, hair barely dry, to a tea dance. Throw in a stroll around to my house for a cup of coffee in the early evening, and he wasn't in any place long enough to get bored.

Dad's low boredom threshold and mania for action drove Mum demented at times. Never more so than the day before I was born, when he managed to lose both his sons in the space of sixty minutes. Mum had gone into hospital to prepare for a Caesarean. It was a lovely warm September day in 1958 and Dad decided to drive the family out to Frensham Pond, near our home in Farnborough, for a blast of fresh air. He parked the car and gave Simon, ten, and Andy, eight, strict instructions to be back in exactly an hour's time.

'At three p.m., mind. Not a minute late. If you're not here, I'll go without you,' he blustered as Simon got his new watch out ready to synchronize it with Dad's in time-honoured military fashion.

My brothers tore off to start re-enacting the *Battle of the Bulge*, with Andy as General Patton blazing a path through the bushes and Simon as the entire German army mounting an offensive from halfway up a tree. Fifty minutes later – with the crossword puzzle finished – Dad was impatiently drumming his fingers on the steering wheel, saying to Hilary, who was steadfastly reading *Jane Eyre* on the back seat: 'Where on earth are those daft lads? I don't want to miss visiting hours.'

'They're probably by the pond,' said Hilary. 'That's where they normally play their war games.'

'Great idea. I'll go over there right now and we'll pick them up,' said Dad, thrilled at the prospect of being on the move and doing something.

Hilary, already at twelve the more sensible one of the two of them, was instantly anxious. 'No, Daddy. I didn't mean that. Just wait here. They'll be back soon.'

But Dad was already off. A few minutes later, he had parked up and was wandering around the lake calling out to the American and German platoons that it was time to pack up and come home for tea.

'I can't see them anywhere. Where can they be?' he said, as he stomped back to the car.

'Well, Daddy,' said Hilary, wearily putting down her book and looking at her watch. 'You never know, they might even be back where you told them to be and wondering where the car is because, right now, it's one minute past three.'

'Kerrrips, kerrrumbs. It never is,' said Dad – using one of his all-time favourite Dadisms. He dived into the car and roared back to the car park. But no one was there.

'They'll be here in a minute, won't they, Hilary? Those daft lads are always late. They'll turn up,' said Dad hopefully.

But they didn't turn up. They were already on the road, marching home at the double. My brothers had staggered back, battle-weary, just a few minutes late, and when they couldn't see the car, they believed that Dad had done exactly what he'd threatened to do, and had left without them. Seizing command of the situation, Simon decided there was only one thing for it. They would have to march the eight miles home. And so they did.

'That silly clown,' Dad recalls, shaking his head in bewilderment. 'He didn't realize that I'd just been giving them a yarn.'

I see his point. Dad has never been a strict disciplinarian. And Simon has always been very literal-minded.

For the next two hours, Dad combed the woods, anxiously quizzing everyone in sight, even roping in the police to join in the hunt. When he wasn't panicking about what had happened to the boys, he was frantically trying to work out how he could break the news to Mum that he'd managed to lose half their family in the space of a single afternoon. He still didn't know what to say when finally he broke off from the hunt and drove full pelt to the hospital with Hilary, tearing up the stairs just as visiting hours finished.

'Hi, darling, all well?' Dad gasped, all wild eyes and flustered face.

Just one look and Mum smelt a rat. Perhaps it was a good thing that she was already half-crazed on sedating drugs, because she started barking up totally the wrong tree.

'I've been out of my mind with worry,' she wailed. 'How could you abandon me like this? I know what you've been up to. You've spent the afternoon with Audrey next door.'

Dad, the most faithful of husbands, was dumbfounded – particularly as Mum, the most rational of women, had never been given to wild flights of jealousy. But he had such a guilty conscience about the terrible crime he'd actually committed that he instantly flushed bright red. Heaven alone knows how it would have ended if the ward sister hadn't arrived just at that moment to announce that visiting hours were over. Dad was ushered out, calling protestations of love over his shoulder, which went some way to reassure Mum.

With his heart in his mouth, he drove back home. There was Andy, asleep on the doormat. Simon was in the garden, playing with his bow and arrow. It had taken them three hours to reach home.

'I hoped I'd never have to tell Mum that I'd been such a fool,' Dad admits. 'But poor Andy was so exhausted that I kept him off school the next day, and when Mum found out, I had to tell her the whole story.'

Dad's ageing seems to dismay me far more than it does him. I don't want him to lose his verve and vigour. I don't want him to lose his grip on life. But I can sense it happening. Although there isn't the faintest sniff of senility, there are a great many things that Dad simply can't be bothered about any more. He has never been very hot on names. It was a standing joke that all the girls he ever taught were called Flossie, and all the boys were Johnnie. But now there are times when I mention a name and it draws a total blank.

Although he sees Rebecca most evenings, he finds it impossible to remember her name. One evening she arrives with her beautiful blond bob dyed magenta-red.

'What on earth have you done that for, you silly lass?' Dad joshes. Mercifully, Rebecca takes it in good part, but I realize this might be a chance to make her name stick once and for all.

The next evening, as we wait for her arrival after supper, he claims total ignorance of her name. So I remind him: 'She's Rebecca with the red hair – Red Rebecca.'

Dad grins. 'Ah yes, daft lass.'

We seem to have cracked it. She's Red Rebecca. Dad's

pleased with himself. I'm relieved. And then comes the day when Rebecca suddenly dies her hair blond again. That's it. I am, as Dad would put it, 'snookered'. I don't even try to get Dad to remember 'Blonde Becky'. There are only so many permutations I can go through – and certainly not as many as there are hair shades.

He knows Laura's name, of course. But even so, he doesn't always remember it. I cringe when he calls out 'Pyjama Girl'. But she doesn't seem to mind.

'I answer to anything as long as it's not rude,' she says, smiling.

Right from the start Dad christened his carers Pyjama Girls. It amused him to have this bevy of lovely young women helping him in and out of his pyjamas. What better job title? The name has stuck so firmly that Dad has completely forgotten they are officially 'carers', and now he routinely refers to his 'Pyjama Girls' as though it's the most natural thing in the world.

His thirst for knowledge and his tenacity were the stuff of family folklore. Terrier-like, once he had the scent, he would crash around the bushes, charging in and out of every rabbit hole in his mind until he grasped the fact, the memory or the answer to a crossword puzzle. Ask him a question and he would shut his eyes and think and think until it came to him. Which it nearly always did. I didn't need Google. I had Dad.

'I don't suppose you can remember the name of the character in Charles Dickens's *David Copperfield* who pretended to be terribly humble, can you, Dad?' I rang to ask one night when I was up against a deadline, writing an article about a new TV production of the novel.

I could almost hear the click, click of Dad racking his brains. Ten minutes later, he rang back, voice full of excited satisfaction.

'Uriah Heep,' he blurted out.

'I beg your pardon?'

'Uriah Heep – the man who was ever so 'umble. You wanted to know.'

'Brilliant, Dad. Thanks. So did you find it in the book?' I asked.

I might as well have accused Dad of cheating. He sounded hurt. 'I didn't need to do that. It came to me eventually. Made me think, though, I ought to read *David Copperfield* again. Wonderful writer, Dickens.'

Dad was also a whizz at sums. When I bought a house after my first divorce, it was Dad who helped organize the mortgage, comparing a plethora of interest rates and repayment terms. It may sound daft but, in my entire life, I have never quite understood how percentages work. I've never needed to – because Dad has always been happy to help.

The first sign of Dad slowing down was when he stopped reading. 'I can't make out the print,' he said, pointing in frustration at his copy of Shakespeare's *Twelfth Night*. No wonder: it was a copy inherited from Mum's parents. The pages were as thin as tracing paper. The print was brown with age.

I ordered Dad a brand-new copy on Amazon. But he still couldn't manage. So, three months after Dad moved in, we went to the optician's. He recognized the problem instantly. Dad had cataracts in both eyes.

'Ah, I remember now. The optician did mention there was a slight problem last time I came,' said Dad.

I was shocked. It was so unlike Dad not to get things seen to instantly.

'I suppose I forgot,' he shrugged apologetically. I couldn't blame him. So much had happened in the last year.

The doctor duly confirmed the diagnosis and Dad was booked in for operations. Taking him to the hospital, I felt strangely protective. Dad was in a wheelchair, on long-term loan from the Red Cross. As we sat in the waiting area, it felt like having a baby in a pram as I fussed over where to position him. Beside me? In front of me? Dad's deafness added to his vulnerability.

I'd explained to Dad that it was a very quick operation, but I'm not sure he believed me. When he was all done and ready to go home within the hour, he was hugely impressed.

'Wow. That's real service,' he announced approvingly. 'And they say I'll be able to see again in a few days once it's all settled down. Super.'

It really was fantastic. But although the operation was a success and Dad got new glasses, which meant he could read again, it didn't have the effect I'd expected. The *Sunday Times* crossword, which had been his weekly ritual since time immemorial, lay barely touched beside his armchair.

Books piled up on the table, unread. Gradually, the truth dawned: Dad was losing interest in the world outside him. He was still eager to know what the girls and I and the rest of the family were up to. But the History Channel no longer had him riveted with attention. He even stopped trying to drag me in to watch *Deal or No Deal* with him. It really upset me.

'So what do you do, Dad, if you don't read and you're not really interested in watching TV?' I asked.

'I think.'

'But what about?'

'The past.'

'And what in the past?'

'I suppose I think a lot about Mum and about Hilary and about all the happy times.'

Hilary? Happy times? That really surprised me. I have never liked to think about Hilary, because thinking about her makes me sad. And remembering happy times with her makes me saddest of all. I don't want to remember lying in the bath, agog, as she told me the entire story of Agatha Christie's *The Mirror Crack'd From Side to Side,* which she'd just been reading. I don't want to remember her carrying me all the way home after we went blackberry picking and I had fallen in the brambles. I don't want to remember hiding under the bedclothes when I was Peter Rabbit and she was Benjamin Bunny and Simon, with an almost impenetrable Scottish accent, was Mr McGregor, prodding and poking the blanket and threatening such dire tortures that I almost wet myself with fear. And I most especially don't want to remember the night before her wedding when she crept into the bedroom that we shared and fibbed that she'd love me best forever.

But Dad's eyes take on a faraway look as he starts telling me about my sister as a little girl.

'I was away from home after she was born, you know. I was up in Preston for thirteen months doing a teacher training course while Mum and Hilary were back home in Birmingham. She was only twelve months old and I missed her terribly, so I made her a doll's house.'

'A doll's house? Wasn't she a bit young?' Then I remember Dad's impatience. Of course, he wouldn't have been able to wait.

'I'd always promised myself that, if I had a little girl, she would have a doll's house. It was the one thing in the world my sister Bessie wanted.'

Bessie, who was just eleven months older than Dad, was his constant companion when they were children.

'Bessie never got one, of course. She used to go and play with a little girl up the road, an only child, who had everything that opened and shut. Bessie would come back from playing with that doll's house and talk of nothing else for days. So that's what I wanted for Hilary.

'Wood was hard to get hold of in 1947, but I found a shop selling bits of timber and I managed to buy some ply wood. I didn't have a plan to follow, but it was quite straightforward. I decorated the interior with wallpaper and paint. It was huge, so getting it back home was a problem. Luckily, one of the other lads had a car and he gave a few of us a lift home. I travelled all the way from Preston to Birmingham with this blessed doll's house on my lap.

'Mum made carpets and curtains from scraps of material and we gave it to Hilary for Christmas. I can see her now. The front came off and it was so big that she could almost crawl inside it. All the family gave her little bits of furniture. She was pleased as punch.'

I check to see if Dad's eyes are misting over at the memory like mine are. But he's smiling to himself and I can see that, for him, it's December 1947 all over again. And nothing that came later mars his joy in the memory. I find it hard to understand. For me, the past is so painful, I'd erase it all if I could. But it haunts me.

When I was ill, I used to make a stupid joke that my life divided into two halves – BC (Before Cancer) and AD (After Diagnosis). Like Dad, I found it comforting to reminisce about events BC. It gave me hope that I would one day be that woman again, living that life.

How can I describe chemotherapy? It was the fluorescent orange of Sunny Delight and smelt of the Johnson's baby shampoo I'd been trickling on to my hair to try and stop it falling out. And it was so powerful that when I weed, it came out red. Everything I ate tasted like rusty metal, and when I tried to lift my head from the pillow it felt like it had been nailed down. The nurses in the special chemo suite were as relentlessly upbeat as the band that went down with the *Titanic*. There was a fish pond, a biscuit tin and a coffee machine in the waiting room – along with leaflets on how to cope if the cancer came back and fliers for natty head-scarves. And there was a library of DVDs you could order up to watch from the comfort of your La-Z-Boy-style arm-chair as the chemo was dripped into your veins.

But nothing, absolutely nothing, could make the experi-ence less ghastly. Richard offered to sit with me for that first session. Then he got out his glasses and opened his newspaper.

'I want you to talk to me,' I wailed, desperate for dis-traction.

But, put on the spot, Richard didn't know what to say. I longed for him to make me laugh, to reminisce about happy times: taking the girls hunting for dinosaur footprints in the Isle of Wight; being at the Globe Theatre for Mark Rylance's *Twelfth Night* when at the very moment Feste started singing 'The rain it raineth every day' the heavens opened; discovering the best ice-cream shop in Venice and trying out a different flavour every single day; taking the girls' hamsters on holiday with us and the drama when they escaped and ate the carpet in our holiday chalet. Instead, Richard started reading aloud from the paper – a doom-laden article about a threatened slump in property prices. It might have vaguely interested me once. But it certainly didn't now.

'Don't worry,' I sighed. 'Just go. Honestly, there's no need for you to hang around here. I'll be fine.'

He seemed reluctant to leave, but I imagined that he wanted to be anywhere but here in this room with these sick people who brought back memories of his own illness and fears which he believed he'd long since eradicated. How could I blame him? This was tough for me. But it wasn't easy for him either.

On the rare occasions when we talked about death, he was glibly dismissive. 'Promise me you will look after the girls,' I said, trying not to imagine how hard it would be for him to raise teenage daughters, but utterly confident that he would always be scrupulously fair and do the right thing by them. 'And if you marry again, please, please make sure she loves the girls, too.'

He looked horrified. 'Darling, you know there's no way I'll ever marry again. I love you. I'll never want anyone else.'

'But you won't want to be celibate for the rest of your life,' I argued. 'And I don't expect it. You're young. You'll want a new life.'

Richard shuddered. 'I don't ever think about it. Besides, I'm in no doubt you're going to outlive me. You'll be playing the merry widow when I'm long in my grave.'

So there I was, a drip trickling chemo into my hand, a copy of *Middlemarch* on my lap, trying to avoid looking at the other women in the room, hooked up to their own drips with skin pale as cement, goggle-eyed, tiny wisps of hair around their bald heads. How could they bear to look like this? And then I realized that we had no choice.

Back home that night, Richard fussed around me. He'd made the bed up with fresh sheets and when I said that the only food I craved was spicy guacamole – heaven alone knows why – he disappeared into the kitchen to make me up a big bowl of it. He ran me a bath, and when it was time for bed, he led me there by the hand.

But it was a text from Peter that really cheered me up. 'How are you, old girl? Thank God you had the foresight to build that vomitarium,' he quipped. I kept expecting to feel sick – it's what everyone warns you about with chemo. But the powerful anti-nausea drugs I'd been prescribed seemed to work. However, I felt wrung out and disorientated – as though I'd just flown in from Australia with a howling six-month-old baby on one side and a jibbering junkie going cold turkey on the other, and with a couple of stopovers thrown in for good measure. My head hammered, my shoulders and arms ached. I was exhausted, but my brain was racing because of the steroids I'd been given to improve the effectiveness of the chemo.

I went through the same procedure every two weeks all the way through June and July. Each session was harder as my body got weaker and weaker and the poor abused vein in my hand throbbed in pain every time the needle came near it.

When I was healthy and had choices, I took so many things for granted: sitting in a chair without feeling weak and queasy; strolling to the post box without needing a sit down; walking around the supermarket without finding the colours so garish and the smells so overpowering that I had to abandon my trolley and wobble outside; lying in the bath without recoiling at the sight of my maimed body.

The list of indignities went on and on. Losing the hair on my head was horrible, but, in some ways, losing my body hair was every bit as devastating. My eyelashes were now a few stray hairs. Every single pubic hair had fallen out. When I looked in the mirror, I saw a cross between a freakish pre-pubescent child and a Belsen victim – hairless, ribcage jutting out where my breast used to be. I barely felt human. And I certainly didn't feel feminine. How could I, when the longest hair on my body sprouted from under my armpit?

Dad must have noticed my physical deterioration. But he never said anything and treated me the same as he'd always done. We still tried to have him around for lunch every Sunday, but now it was Richard who did the cooking. And sometimes when he came for coffee in the week, it would be Richard, not me, who chatted to him because I was too tired.

When the girls were out of earshot, and I was alone with Richard, I cried and wailed. He was the only one I could trust with my terror and self-loathing, and I clung to him like a limpet.

The one other person who understood was my new friend, Anne. We'd met in adjoining hospital beds and I'd immediately warmed to her mixture of kindness, gutsiness and schoolgirl humour. She'd been a music teacher, then a housemistress at Winchester College, and while she had a touching willingness to see the best in everyone and every situation, years of staying one step ahead of the cocky young boys in her charge had given her a shrewd insight into human nature. She had two daughters who had just finished university, and when I discovered that her marriage had ended shortly before she was diagnosed, I found myself wanting to cry and – for the first time since this whole wretched business started – I wasn't crying for me.

We leant on each other. We laughed together. We teased each other and we shared intimacies I would never have dreamt of discussing even with my oldest friends.

'OK, here's a question for you and I want an honest answer. What's worse – losing the hair up here –' I gestured '– or down there?'

We were sipping coffee in Starbucks, so absorbed in the nitty-gritty of what we were going through that we were oblivious to anyone around us.

Anne had managed to cling on to some of her lovely brunette bob. She wore it with an Alice band which helped to mask the bald patches. Even so, it looked lank and some-how dead. But I wasn't about to let her know that. And when she pointed at her hair and grimaced, I rushed to reassure her.

'It still looks lovely,' I said. 'You're so lucky. All your own hair. Both breasts.'

Anne laughed: 'Don't think you can play the sympathy card with me, madam, when you've got that lovely Richard.'

And then she went all serious. 'Honestly, Tessa. You don't know what I'd give to have someone to give me a hug when I'm feeling lonely and frightened in the middle of the night.' What could I possibly say, because, yes, I did feel incredibly blessed. Richard didn't hug me much any more, but he was there for me and always would be.

But it must have been exhausting for him, I reasoned. So when he asked if I was happy for him to go to the Caribbean again to sort a few minor repairs on Karen's property before the winter season, I agreed. I recognized all that he did for me and I wanted him to have some time out. I was also keen to support his business and these trips were work-related.

'Well, if you are absolutely sure, Tessa,' he said. 'But I'll only go if you are feeling well. And, if anything changes, I'll cancel. No question.'

'And you're sure it's OK about the plane ticket?' I argued, determined to be fair to the woman who was doing my husband such a favour by giving him work that seemed to make him feel good about himself. 'I wouldn't want Karen to lose money.'

'Don't worry, darling. She quite understands. She knows you're in the middle of treatment and I might have to back out at the last minute. She's fine with that. And honestly, a plane ticket's not a lot of money to her.'

By the time Richard left for the Caribbean, it was the end of August. I was exhausted after four bouts of chemo over two and a half months. And I was frightened about how I'd cope without Richard, particularly at night when visions of death haunted me. But I didn't try and persuade him to stay. I wanted to believe I was well enough to cope. And I guess he must have believed me, because when the taxi arrived at 4 a.m. to take him to Gatwick, I kissed him goodbye in the half-light and I didn't cry. I cried afterwards – in the hospital car park as I waited to see my oncologist before starting my new round of chemotherapy. Instead of liquid chemo, shot into my veins, I would be taking tablets every day for the next two months – or at least for as long as my body could manage it. I would take them at home – so no more hideous hospital visits – and the side-effects were much less severe. In fact, my hair would even start growing back.

I should have been pleased, but I wanted Richard there beside me to help decipher things, to help keep me calm. I had come to rely on him more than I realized. Without him I was scared. When Dr Hall, a lovely, wise lady with big glasses and long grey hair in a neat bun, who always made me think of Harry Potter's Transfiguration teacher, Professor McGonagall, asked how I was, I started crying all over again.

'I'm really frightened. I can't get my head around what's happened and I'm so scared the cancer's going to come back.'

Dr Hall didn't ignore my fears. She didn't brush them aside or, even worse, admit that I had every reason to be fearful. Instead, she did something totally unexpected. She quoted T. S Eliot.

'Do you know the line: "The tense is everything"? You did have a cancerous tumour, my dear. But it is now gone. As far as anyone knows, nothing else is happening.'

'The tense is everything.' I wanted to hug her. I wanted to rush home and tell Richard. But I couldn't. He rang twice a day and sent loving texts. I've kept them. There they are on my phone. 'Hello, darling. How are you? Missing you and the girls. xxx' I've kept them because there's a tiny part of me that still needs the proof to believe this all really happened.

One evening, when the girls were out, I went over to Dad's to watch the film *The Queen* on TV. Simon was staying. Sweetly, he had understood that I didn't have the energy to entertain Dad as much as I had before I was ill and wanted to share some of the load. Watching them potter around Dad's flat was like a rerun of *The Odd Couple*. Dad all doilies, teapots and sugar bowls like Jack Lemmon; Simon doing a fine impression of Walter Matthau, plonking mugs and whisky glasses anywhere but on Dad's coasters and leaving a trail of crumpled newspapers and magazines on every available surface. He and Dad made a huge fuss of me in their rather cackhanded way. There were endless cups of tea, Mr Kipling jam tarts and Jamaica ginger cake – all Dad's favourites, which he fondly believed everyone must love every bit as much as he did. Sitting there in my wig, sipping tea and knitting (a hobby my friend Bridget had encouraged me to revive while I was having treatment), I thought how lovely it was to feel pampered. Dad never once asked about the cancer, but all the little gestures – jumping up to pour me an extra cup of tea, insisting that Simon walk me home, and pressing a box of Black Magic chocolates into my hands (actually my sister's favourites, not mine, but I'd never had the heart to tell Dad) made me feel safe for the first time since Richard had left for the Caribbean.

And for the first time I admitted to myself that, even though I'd encouraged Richard to go, I wished he hadn't gone. No wonder that I was trying to tell myself and every-one else that he had gone for the money and to get some time alone. Seeing me unwell and caring for me must have been upsetting and tiring. Deep down, I was upset and should have told him not to go. However vociferously I denied it, I needed him here with me.

Until now, it had seemed that we were in this cancer thing together. Richard and Tessa versus Breast Cancer. Now, with Richard on the other side of the world, it struck me for the first time that it was my problem and mine alone. It felt as if my life was in jeopardy. Although he was sympathetic, Richard was able to carry on virtually as normal. This was never more apparent than when he was spending time wind-surfing or in the Caribbean. I felt myself harden towards him just a fraction. When he'd been away before, I had made sure that I was there to welcome him back and make a fuss of him. This time, I deliberately arranged for my friend Shelly to come for coffee at around the time I expected Richard home. I wanted to prove to myself and to him that life went on very nicely without him, thank you very much. Forgetting that I had encouraged him to go, it suddenly felt as if, by going to the Caribbean, that's exactly the point he had been making to me.

Richard seemed on edge when the taxi deposited him at our front door. I put it down to the fact that he was tired after his long flight and that he hadn't expected to walk in on a coffee party. But there was still a sense of distance that evening after he'd woken from his nap. Maybe my feelings were rubbing off on him. Instead of the wonderful reunion I'd spent the last week longing for, we ended up squabbling.

'It's been an awful week. You can't imagine how lonely and miserable I've been,' I complained.

'But you had your dad and the girls and I rang every day,' he countered.

'It's not the same and you know it. You abandoned me!'

'That's really not fair, Tessa. You told me to go. If you'd asked me to stay, you know that I would have.' He sounded frustrated.

'But I shouldn't have had to plead with you to stay. You should have wanted to.'

'I'm sorry. But Tessa, you're doing so well, you really don't need me.'

'I do, I do,' I wailed, and huge tears plopped on to my man's shirt like a cartoon character's. I didn't know whether it was excess of emotion or shortage of eyelashes, but nowadays my tears fell like huge, perfectly formed drops of water.

And I really did need Richard. The capecitabine tablets were beginning to have hideous effects on my skin. My hands and feet were red and sore – as though the skin had been stretched. Walking was becoming painful. And every day the side-effects intensified. By the time Richard had been back two weeks, my hands were bright red. They looked as though they'd been boiled in cooking oil. Even turning on a tap hurt. When I walked into the bathroom, treading on a crack between the floorboards made me wince in pain as though I was walking on the edge of a knife.

One morning at the beginning of October, I got out of the bath to find the skin peeling off my feet in great sheets like wallpaper. It was grotesque. There's a wonderful but deeply disturbing painting by Titian – *The Flaying of Marsyas*. The foolish satyr challenged the god Apollo to a music contest. When he lost, Apollo had him flayed alive, stripping skin from his body, inch by awful inch. Now my body was flaying me from the inside. First the cancer. Then the hair loss. Now this. It had betrayed me yet again. The only bright spot was that my hair had started growing back. It was half a centimetre long. And it was growing all over! I grabbed Elise the second she came in from school. 'Look, I've got a hair growing on my chin,' I squealed. Unaccountably, she failed to share my excitement. But the thrill was indescribable.

My first radiotherapy session was in the diary for 1 November. A fifteen-minute dose, five days a week until 21 November. It would be the last leg of this whole horrible treatment. By the time it finished I would have lived with cancer for nine months – as long as it takes to grow a baby.

Richard drove me to Southampton General Hospital to discuss what was in store. The oncology wing was bright and airy with soothing pictures of French seaside villages on the walls – all blue skies and bougainvillaea. Carefully, the nurse started explaining the procedure. First I would be marked with a tattoo pen so that they would be able to target precisely where to direct the beams. The marks would be black and tiny, she reassured me. But they would be permanent. I didn't like to think of it – permanent blackheads in my cleavage and armpit.

'We'll also mark the area where your breast was,' she said breezily.

Was? Was? The tense is everything. And the past tense was like a kick in the guts. Of course she was right. My breast had gone. Had I really thought it was only temporarily mislaid? That I'd find it again? How long would it take before I accepted the truth? My breast was never coming back. I was never going to be whole again.

As I tried to take in all the nurse had told me, the lovely Dr Hall appeared. She took one of my hands in hers. It was such a vicious red that it looked like a slab of meat. The skin had peeled off the tips of my fingers.

'I think you've had enough, my dear,' she said, gently. 'We'll stop the chemotherapy.'

'What now? But I've got two more doses to go,' I gulped.

I should have been ecstatic. Instead, I started crying. Richard looked baffled. But Dr Hall understood.

'It can be such an anti-climax,' she said. She was right.

I'd had my chemo end date – 26 October – virtually engraved on my heart. I was like a long-distance athlete who reaches the finishing line half a mile up the road. I wasn't ready. But it wasn't just that. All the suppressed emotion and the shock I'd buried so deep was pouring out now that I dared let it. I wanted to sob and sob. I'd done it. I'd got to the end.

Back home, Richard suggested celebrating with champagne, but I feared it would just make me even more weepy. Besides, the chemotherapy was still playing havoc with my taste buds. Champagne, dry white wine – they tasted like vinegar. Bizarrely, I'd developed a liking for sweet sherry. So I sat in the armchair in front of the Aga and sipped sherry while Richard fussed over me.

By the next day, I was feeling more cheerful and eager to prove to myself that I was ready to join the world of normal people. It was half-term and I decided to do the most normal thing I could think of – take the girls shopping. I was nervous and I'd have liked Richard to come, but he was working. So I drove alone with the girls to West Quay shopping centre in Southampton. It was only twelve miles away but it seemed such a momentous undertaking, I might as well have been setting off for Antarctica. I hadn't driven further than the few familiar streets around our home since I had been diagnosed and I felt very vulnerable. There were so many cars. They were going so fast and they all seemed to be heading towards me. My knuckles were white on the steering wheel by the time I finally reached the multi-storey car park and launched the car into the largest space I could find. Somewhere along the line, like when I was pregnant, I seemed to have completely lost any sense of spatial awareness. I was shaking when we walked into the shopping centre. I clung to Elise. The noise, the colours, the smells were all so overpowering that I felt faint. I was toddling around like a decrepit visitor from a distant age. I was Tess of the d'Urbevilles catapulted from the wilds of Wessex into Top Shop. I caught a glimpse of myself in a mirror and stood rooted to the spot in shock. I looked like a middle-aged mum spaced out on cocaine.

Richard drove me to my first radiotherapy session early in the afternoon of 1 November. I was tense with nerves. As the nurse talked me through the procedure again, she made it all sound easy. All I had to do was lie down and relax while the radiotherapy beam was shot at my chest. Easy – unless you think about it too deeply. Phil Collins was on the stereo as the nurses eased me into position on the bed. It felt as though I was being lined up for a lunar landing. 'Up a bit. Down a bit. No, up a bit more. Slide across a fraction. Now down a bit. We're good to go.'

On the ceiling there was a soothing back-lit picture of trees in autumn colours. Apparently, there were six separate radiotherapy rooms, all with different scenes. I looked at the picture and tried to imagine a day when I'd be walking through the forest, revelling in the colours, exulting in the last rays of sun. Next year, perhaps. Would I really? Could I imagine it? The nurse coming into the room shook me out of my reverie. The whole process had taken just seven minutes.

But that night I broke down as I started to rub my chest with cream to stop my skin, reddened from the radiotherapy, from peeling. It was the first time I had touched my chest since the operation – six months ago. I had come to accept my reflection in the mirror. But this horrible bony chest, like a cutlery drawer where all the forks are pointing out, felt revolting.

Shopping for socks for Richard in Marks and Spencer the following week, I managed to walk past the lingerie department without blubbing. But the effort of keeping my emotions under control had exhausted me. My oldest friend Dominique had offered to drive me to radiotherapy sessions once a week. Today was her slot. Dominique has a mania for being on time, so we arrived thirty minutes early for my session. I was so exhausted that I felt like curling up and going to sleep while poor Domi valiantly tried to make small talk. I lay on the couch while the two nurses lined me up, and I started crying – very softly to begin with. I'd been trying so hard to hide from breast cancer, but it had caught up with me. I found myself dwelling on what was really happening. Radiotherapy rays were being shot into my sad, maimed skin. They were so powerful that the nurses couldn't even be in the room while I had the treatment. As the nurses left and the lights dimmed, warm tears started soaking into my ears. I wanted to cry even harder. The dark, womb-like room seemed so comforting. But I knew cameras were trained on me. The nurses could see everything. What would they think? How could I let myself down like this? As I got dressed I noticed a huge wet stain on my shoe. It was a tear. One of the nurses tried to comfort me.

'This is so hard, but you know you can have a massage or some relaxation therapy, if you'd like,' she said. 'It might make you feel a lot better.'

I nodded my head mutely. Her kindness made me want to cry even more. In the car, Dominique did her best to comfort me. In so many ways, we know each other inside out. We have been friends since our first year at senior school, and apart from the odd blip – like the time I got us sacked from school tuck-shop duty by fighting with a customer – we've never fallen out. But until I got ill I didn't realize how much Domi mattered to me. Or how far she'd go to help me. She hugged me. If I tell you that Domi and I had never in thirty-eight years hugged, you will know just what a significant moment it was. And I cried even more.

Back home, Dominique came in for a drink. Seeing my tears, Richard rushed to kiss me and stroke my back. 'There, there, darling,' he said, and I clung to him for dear life.

When I think about that time, it's totally overshadowed by the horror waiting in the wings. In fact, I actively avoid thinking about anything that happened in the first period, because it's all been poisoned by what happened next. It's Before Richard's Affair and After Richard's Affair. I wish I could think of an antidote to draw the poison out of it, but I can't.

Every happy memory from those passionate falling-in-love years is polluted by what came afterwards. Every time I'm tempted to look back at the beginning of the story, the end comes crashing in to trash my dreams. A dark stain trickles into every crevice of my life with Richard.

Yet the truth is, I know that, whatever happened at the end, I was really happy for many, many years. So was Richard. There wasn't a single portent of disaster at the beginning. If I missed any clues, they were tiny ones. Our marriage should have gone the distance. If I could only bury all the sadness and bitterness, I might actually find a way to see the past clearly. How does Dad do it? He so clearly gets genuine pleasure from remembering Hilary.

Dad seems surprised when I ask him the question. 'But Tetty, love,' he says. 'Why would I want to deprive myself of happy memories? What happened, happened. But it doesn't stop me thinking about Hilary. She was my little girl and I never want to forget how much I loved her and how proud and happy she made me. In fact, I love to think about her.

'She was the first member of the family to go to university. You probably don't understand just how much that meant to us. I'd left school at fourteen without a single qual-ification. Mum had a brilliant mind, but she wouldn't go to university because it meant being dependent on the old man and she couldn't bear that. And there was Hilary going to Oxford. When she got in, I was so chuffed. It caused a lot of resentment, you know. There were all these majors and colonels sending their children to the best private schools and they couldn't understand why their kids didn't get into Oxford when Hilary did. Some colonel's wife even had the cheek to complain to Mum that it wasn't fair. Well, you know how Mum could never dissemble. She just looked at her and said: "Wouldn't it be wonderful if we could all buy brains for our children?"'

I laugh. So like my mum. And then I think what pleasure I get from thinking about her, how important it is to talk to the girls about the grandmother they only dimly remember. She might be dead, but I refuse to bundle her off the scene. She made me who I am. And, in a very real way, I have to acknowledge that for the eleven years I lived with and loved Richard, he, too, helped shape me. Perhaps never more so than in the last few months. To deny that is to deny a very real part of who I am now. Whatever happened in the end, there were very many things that were good and genuine and lovely about our relationship. Would I have chosen never to have fallen in love with him, just so that I could avoid the pain of the ending?

I look at Dad, deep in his reverie of life with Hilary and Mum, and I see how impossible it is to root out the memory of genuine love, however painful it may be at times. Why would I want to forget that I once loved so much and was loved so deeply in return?

SEVEN

VALUING EVERY DAY

When my chemotherapy ended, it was as though the curtain had been whisked back and I'd been dragged on to the stage and straight into the chorus line of *Mamma Mia!* – all 100-watt smiles, high kicks and backflips. I was in a constant state of high alert for fun, and never more so than when I could find a legitimate reason to celebrate. What better reason than our tenth wedding anniversary on 8 November 2007?

The date coincided with the halfway mark of my month of radiotherapy sessions. Richard had booked a table at a new restaurant. Reservations were like gold dust. I was really excited. Not just about the restaurant, not just about the fact that it was a milestone anniversary, but because I hadn't been, out in public at night with Richard in five months. I'd felt too fragile and too exhausted. And seeing people like I'd once been, carelessly enjoying themselves like I'd once done, would have made me rancid with envy. But now, venturing into the grown-up world of healthy adults felt like a step back to becoming fully human again. Wearing my wig and carefully made-up to disguise the fact that I still had only a few stray eyebrows and barely a single eyelash, I believed I could pass for the old me.

Sitting opposite Richard, savouring every mouthful of exquisite roast lamb and dauphinoise potatoes, I looked back on how I used to imagine celebrating our tenth wedding anniversary. I'd craved a stonking diamond ring. That's what so many of my friends had. And I envied them. However often I told myself that it wasn't Richard's fault that he'd given up life in the City and a large income to live in Winchester with me, I couldn't help but harbour a niggling resentment. It didn't help that I could see that he wasn't happy, either. Or that I found it hard not to make unfavourable comparisons with my energetic dad.

The days have never been long enough for Dad to pack in all he wants to do. And time has rarely passed fast enough for him not to get bored. Our homes were regularly put up for sale on a whim and just as rapidly taken off the market when Dad's enthusiasm for a tumbledown DIY project in the New Forest or a windblown apartment by the sea came up against the chill reality of surveyors' reports and mortgage assessments. I'd bump along in the back of the car on house-hunting forays, excitedly pointing out 'Free Houses' and wondering why they had peculiar names like 'The Goose and Gander' or 'The Horse and Jockey' while my world-weary siblings tittered.

Small wonder, perhaps, that Dad's favourite poem has

always been 'The Pedlar's Caravan', a sickly, sentimental Victorian children's poem he learnt in infant school along with John Masefield's 'Sea Fever'. Whenever Dad recited 'I wish I lived in a caravan, with a horse to drive, like the pedlar man', it was with an eager glint in his eye. Sometimes Mum got caught up in Dad's madcap enthusiasms, or maybe it was more that she didn't have the energy or the heart to stamp too harshly on his latest dream. In one giddy seven-year period we moved home three times. But, more often than not, Dad relied on Mum to extract him from the latest scrape that his unbounded eagerness and impatience had catapulted him into. In fact, I suspect now that he only allowed himself to roar off on his flights of fancy because he knew there was someone to drag him down to earth.

But now I swept those thoughts aside – I was determined to be happy, and to make Richard happy too. This was my new mission in life and I seized on it like a woman possessed. That night I looked back on that other mean-spirited, materialistic woman that I used to be like an unappealing stranger to be avoided at a party. I felt like I'd downed half a bottle of the best champagne in one glorious gulp, but I'd got all the giddy euphoria and none of the queasiness. Everything was more intense – the chatter of the other diners, the clatter from the kitchen, the glittering of the glasses in the candlelight. The food was divine, the service was just the right side of solici-tous and the wine was sufficiently chilled. That evening I was drunk on the sheer joy that I was sitting here, in a restaurant with my husband, still breathing and actually able to reach

10 p.m. without sinking my head on the table in exhaustion. And when Richard ordered a final glass of champagne for us, I was so happy, I started crying.

'Darling, what is it? Aren't you feeling well? Shall we go home?' he asked, all tender concern.

'It's because I'm so happy and I love you so much,' I gulped. 'You've been so good to me. I couldn't have got through this without you.'

Richard reached for my hand. Tears were welling up in his eyes too. 'Darling, I've done nothing. You're the one who's been through hell. You've been so brave.'

I didn't feel brave. But I did feel wonderfully, supremely blessed. I had the girls. I had Richard. I could see the end of the treatment. I could see the start of a new life and I was determined it would be nothing like the old one. I woke every morning with the wild-eyed glee of a marathon runner, desperate to hit the road, terrified of being left on the starting block while the race tore on without me.

'I don't want to die with things undone' became my mantra. It must have irritated the hell out of people, but I was so supercharged on serotonin, so self-absorbed in the joy of being well, that I carried on regardless. Richard didn't really join in. In fact, he seemed quite distant, but I decided that it was because he was quietly giving me room to enjoy my moment. In any case, I was too swept up to give it much thought. I felt lucky to be alive and I refused to let that go unacknowledged.

I became focused on grabbing every opportunity that came my way. How else would I have found myself appearing on *Dickinson's Real Deal*? I had got addicted to the programme when I was ill. The predictable format was surprisingly soothing. Members of the public turned up with old treasures wrapped in copies of the *Sun* or plastic bags from Iceland. Sometimes they were heirlooms – china cups left to old retainers by grateful squires in the eighteenth century; paintings brought back from Grand Tours by distant ancestors and consigned to the attic in place of Iron Maiden posters. More often they were from car boot sales or charity shops. Everyone claimed not to have a clue about their value. Led into the chirpily named Dealer's Den, they haggled with the professional antique dealers under the guidance of David Dickinson. I loved David for the fact that everything from his huge cream shoes to his irrepressible jauntiness was larger than life. Watching him every weekday afternoon made me feel that all was right with the world and would be for me too.

So when I discovered that the show was filming an episode in Winchester that December after I finished treatment, I was beside myself with excitement. Richard was bemused. The girls were horrified. I ransacked the house and came up with a heavy gold watch chain complete with a huge gold sovereign and an ivory cigar cutter shaped like a champagne bottle. Richard had inherited them from his father's late cousin. He was more than happy for me to try and make a bit of cash out of them. So, with the girls in tow, off I trotted to the Guildhall where filming was due to take place. I knew the key was to look like a bit of a character. I didn't realize that I didn't need to try. I looked virtually certifiable with hair like a well-trodden doormat. Unaccountably, Richard had persuaded me that I looked better au naturel, so I'd stopped wearing my wig. My hair was an uneven mass of bristles, but I was excited as a teenage boy discovering his first chin hair. The girls tactfully tried to persuade me. 'But we love your wig, Mum. You look so glamorous,' they gushed. But I refused to listen.

Ellen flatly refused to be filmed. Elise, squirming with embarrassment, finally agreed. I didn't even feel guilty. I wanted this and I was going to make it happen. And so we ended up in the Dealer's Den with our gold chain. We'd already had a full briefing from the resident experts behind the scenes to haggle our way to at least £200.

'It belonged to a relative of my husband's,' I explained to dealer, Tim Hogarth, as the cameras started rolling. 'We're very keen to have something to remember her by. We'd thought of having the chain made into two bracelets, but the girls aren't keen. I thought we could sell it and buy something they would each like to wear.'

Trying to ignore just how peculiar I looked, Tim turned to Elise 'So do you have expensive taste?'

'Afraid so,' she said gamely.

Gradually Tim edged his offer up from £150 to £200 with us both egging him on, 'Am I getting there?'

'A bit more effort,' Elise chirped up.

We'd reached stalemate when David came bounding in from around the screen, instantly on our side and urging us to push for £250.

'You don't want a grown man to beg!' Tim hammed it up.

'You don't want two women to weep, do you?' Elise shot back.

We left with £240, David delighted that we had got the 'Real Deal'. '£120 each for the girls. You can go out and buy a nice piece for the girls and think fondly of the aunt who left you the original piece,' he gushed to camera, while we nodded happily beside him.

I rejoined my Italian class, although I found it frustratingly hard to concentrate. My brain couldn't be bothered to cope with more than one bit of information at a time. Anything too taxing and it kicked up its heels. My friend Anne and I went out for monthly wine-fuelled lunches. We were joined by a mutual friend, Anna, a GP, and two of her friends: Nada and Christine, also doctors. All five of us were either in the last stages of treatment or well down the path to recovery. Defiantly, we called ourselves the Après C club – as in Après Chemotherapy – and swopped stories about all our new adventures, such as Anna's belly-dancing and Anne's renewed passion for travel.

I threw myself into planning treats. One of the first things I did when my radiotherapy ended was arrange a theatre trip with Richard and the girls. It was a West End revival of an Alan Ayckbourn play, *Absurd Person Singular*. Clever. Funny. Great cast – Jane Horrocks, John Gordon

Sinclair, Jenny Seagrove. A love of theatre was one of the major passions Richard and I shared. Momentous events had always been marked by theatre visits. We'd gone to the theatre on our second date (Kevin Whately doing the Henry Fonda decent-man part in *Twelve Angry Men*); we'd slept together for the first time after watching *Richard III*. Hardly Shakespeare's most romantic play, but we were too much in love to care. Richard's first treat for the girls had been an outing to *Beauty and the Beast* in the West End. Aged four and six, they'd been wide-eyed with excitement. We'd last seen a play as a family in February, a week before I was diagnosed. Now I couldn't wait to get back to the theatre. I bought four tickets for the following Saturday, three weeks before Christmas. And then I told Richard, expecting him to enjoy the surprise, but he wasn't keen to keep the long journey up to London.

I was disappointed. But I didn't try to explain why it mattered so much to me. I wanted us to go to the theatre – our special thing – together because my getting there at all would be a milestone. Without him, it just wouldn't be the same. Without him, a lot of things weren't the same. I was becoming dimly aware of the fact that Richard wanted to spend less and less time with me. It's only now, living with Dad, that I can see just how blind I was to what was happening to my marriage. Why didn't I see the signs of Richard's withdrawal? Why didn't I understand the real reason for his trips away?

*

Dad's world has shrunk to the few hundred feet of his bedroom and the garden. There would be every reason for him to behave like a caged lion, thrashing against the bars, desperate to chase the shadows of his old life, bemoaning all the things he can't do any more. That's exactly what I imagined, and I dreaded it. Instead, as he's settled into his gentle new routine, Dad has stunned me by his willingness to find a new way of taking his enjoyment. He rarely seems to hanker after the past. Instead, he determinedly takes his pleasures where he can.

Dad has always loved being outside. Now, as winter gives way to spring, he's itching to get out into the garden at every available opportunity.

'How's the sun doing?' he asks hopefully every morning as he chomps through his morning prunes and porridge. He can sit in the garden for hours, a beatific smile on his face, listening to the birds singing, watching the bees swarming on the lavender and the dog hurling himself in and out of the fuchsia bushes in hunt of imaginary squirrels. 'This is heaven,' he smiles. 'You can't beat sitting in a garden in the sunshine.'

It reminds me of when I was young and Dad would rush home from work, mow the lawn, then sit contemplatively in the dying sunshine with a tankard of home-brewed beer, our cocker spaniel Patsy at his feet. In autumn, he loved bounding around the garden, clearing up leaves and lighting his huge, smelly bonfires. And – come rain or shine – he was out on the golf course every single week.

Summer holidays we spent camping. It had all the elements my parents loved: it was inexpensive, there were no crowds and it meant that Dad could up sticks and move site whenever he fancied. Sometimes he would move pitch just for the fun of it. From our home in Germany, I toured most of Europe with my parents, bunking up every night in a tent outside somewhere like Rome or Vienna before a whistle-stop tour of the city. Dad had bought himself a new camera and was eager to try it out every chance he got. There are photos of me – chocolate ice-cream in hand – outside the Colosseum, the Vatican, the Trevi Fountain and the Palazzo Borghese. Same day. Same city. Different ice-creams.

Mum and Dad carried on camping until well into their sixties – and not because they couldn't afford a swanky holiday in the sun. They carried on because they loved it. They were so reluctant to get rid of the tent and this magical part of their lives that it even resurfaced for their fiftieth wedding anniversary in 1994. With Mum supervising as usual, Dad erected it in their back garden for the party. At night it doubled as an overspill bedroom for my brother Andy and his girlfriend. Celebrating their anniversary in the garden, in their old orange tent, epitomized Mum and Dad's core beliefs: they loathed ostentatious extravagance and they prided themselves on being self-sufficient.

When you're around someone quite so focused on having a good time and making the most of life, it's hard not to get swept along. I find myself eagerly arranging little treats for Dad. At Easter, I throw a family lunch party. Andy and

Simon are staying for the weekend, and I invite our cousin, Maggie and her partner, Peter. Maggie is the daughter of Dad's big sister Bessie and his god-daughter to boot, so they have an especially fond relationship.

Lunch is not exactly a grand affair. Dad's table only seats four, so Andy, Simon and I squash up on his bed, plates of roast lamb on our lap. As we're eating I hear Maggie mention that she's beginning to get aches and pains.

Dad's instantly sympathetic. 'So sorry to hear you've met Arthur (his pet name for 'arthritis'). I bet you wish you hadn't. Anyway, love, welcome to the club.'

One day in early May, I mention that I've seen the first crop of home-grown strawberries in the supermarket. Dad's ears prick up. He's always loved eating fruit in season. He likes it even better if he's picked the fruit himself. He regularly took first me and then the girls to a farm that sold pick-your-own strawberries, raspberries and sweetcorn. Even better – because they're free – Dad has always loved picking blackberries. It comprises two of his greatest pleasures since boyhood: fresh air and the prospect of winning the approval of the woman in his life.

As a child, Dad loved escaping his overcrowded little terrace house in Newcastle and trekking off into the countryside, foraging for blackberries. It would take him all afternoon to find enough decent berries to half fill an old jam jar. When he came home, his mum, normally so harassed, would make a huge fuss of him and get him to help make a blackberry pie. 'Isn't our Jimmy clever?' she would smile as she brought the dish to the table. And Dad would bask in the contentment of making her happy.

With four children to feed and not much money, my mother also appreciated having blackberries she could turn into jam, and blackberry picking became a regular family outing. But I haven't bothered since the girls were tiny. Why on earth waste time when you can get them in Waitrose so easily?

Dad's having none of it. 'What could be nicer than picking your own?' he raves. Then he starts reminiscing about the time he and I had been enthusiastically clearing an entire hedge of blackberries when a chap had suddenly popped up from around the corner. 'Excuse me. These are my blackberries. Would you mind leaving them alone?' he demanded curtly.

Bemused, Dad pointed out that blackberries are a wild fruit and, by definition, no one can lay claim to ownership.

'But these are my blackberry bushes, in my garden,' the man countered, and we suddenly saw the gate in the hedge and the house behind it that we had been far too busy to notice in our eagerness.

Like Dad, Richard used to revel in the tiny pleasures of life. It was one of the qualities I valued in him. But now, I was acutely aware that we weren't sharing any fun times together. He didn't want to go on a trip to New York that I'd excitedly suggested. I couldn't understand it. But I was so cocooned in my own little world of post-cancer exuberance that I batted away the disappointment and ignored the truth that, however much I told myself the illness had brought us closer together, we were in fact growing more and more distant. When another work-related trip to the Caribbean came up, I was furious. I couldn't have been more stunned if he'd slapped me in the face. Yet still I chose to believe that everything was fine, that our marriage was strong.

It's hard not to look back at that woman, hell-bent on seeing the best in every blade of grass, without finding her frankly ludicrous. All the more so when I know how it all ended. How catastrophically the bubble was burst. But while that ecstatic form of joy was often inappropriate, I look at Dad now and I crave to get just a fraction of it back. I don't expect to be able to live every day as if it were my last. That was unsustainable. I remember Mum telling me how, when the war ended, after living for six years on a knife edge, everyone had expected their problems to be over for ever.

'I thought that I would never be unhappy again. We all did,' she explained. 'And for a while, it was like that. Even when we were so poor that I would grapple around in the ashtray hoping Dad might have left a cigarette butt that we could share, I was happy. But you can't stay like that for ever. You have to have light and shade.'

But there's something about knowing, as in really, truly knowing in your heart and your head, that you are going to die one day that should keep you on your toes. It certainly does Dad. Always a glass-three-quarters-full person, it isn't just being close to death that makes Dad so appreciative of all that he still has. Every morning he chooses to focus on all the pleasures he can still find. Even when Dad waves good-night it's with a tender smile on his face.

If Dad knew the expression 'Don't sweat the small stuff', he'd use it – all the time. The things that make me seethe with irritation – the phone left off the charger so long that it's stopped working; the electric toothbrush gummed up with toothpaste; the grimy marks on the girls' bedroom carpets where spattered moisturizer has met months of dust; my black tights disappearing only to return with holes in the toes; tweezers vanishing until my chin's bristling like a porcupine's – they all seem so trivial when set against the force of Dad's irrepressible joie de vivre. When I look hassled, he contemplates me with a mixture of bafflement and sympathy.

'Tetty, love,' he says, 'what are you cross about now? Does it really matter?'

Dad is infinitely more easy-going and tolerant than I am, particularly of the girls. He simply can't understand why I choose to get in such a state of impotent fury about the state of their bedrooms, their habit of eating lunch in their pyjamas and their craze for littering the surface of every room they ever enter with the detritus from their handbags and pockets.

'They're going through a funny time, just like you,' Dad says at the end of one particularly animated rant.

'Like me?' I haven't a clue what he's talking about.

'Well, you're not as young as you were . . . ' his voice tails off. Suddenly, I realize that my dear old dad is talking about the menopause. It's the very last thing I was expecting him to be aware of, let alone mention. And it pulls me up short. He's still very astute and determined to look on the bright side of everything.

The most mundane of things bring him huge pleasure. Dad greets the offer of every cup of tea as if I've suggested high tea at the Savoy. His face crinkles up in delight. 'Ooh, I'd love that,' he enthuses. Throw in a couple of bourbon biscuits and his joy could not be more complete if Laurel and Hardy had popped up to do a turn in the back garden.

One day, after supper, I come into his room to find him sitting in his chair, deep in thought. When I ask him what he's doing, his answer stuns me. 'Just thinking over what a lovely day I've had,' he says.

'But Dad, we haven't really done anything,' I say guiltily.

Dad looks surprised. 'But don't you see, my treasure, it's enough just to wake up in the morning. I'm content in my own little world with you and the family. Why would I want anything more?'

And as Milo races into the room and starts rolling around on the carpet, stretching and yawning and kicking his legs in total doggy abandon, Dad smiles even more broadly.

'Daft dog. He's just rubbing it in that he can do that and I can't.' We both laugh.

EIGHT

BE TRUE TO YOURSELF

When I walk past his open door, I know just from a glance at his head, gently slumped to one side, that Dad's asleep. Now, more often than not, he is.

It didn't really occur to me when Dad moved in but – bizarre as it is – turning our formal sitting room into his bedroom has proved perfect. Anyone who comes in the front door, from the ladies in my book club to the meter reader, walks past his room and its open door. There's always someone to say hello to, to talk to, to make him feel in the midst of things. Some days it must feel as though he's taken up residence under the clock at Waterloo station.

Dad seems to revel in living in a household of three girls: me, Ellen (when she's home from university) and Elise. As far as Dad is concerned, at least two of us are interchangeable, so we'll often answer to each other's names. And we are joined by a constantly evolving cast of characters. Anyone else who turns up is always ceremoniously introduced to Dad. Always chivalrous, Dad has clearly decided it is best to develop the same line for everyone, whatever their age or sex. 'Lovely to meet you. Do forgive me for not getting up.' He finds it hard to keep up to speed with everything going on.

I can see how baffling it must sometimes be for Dad. One of his favourite visitors is Dominique – not only because she always arrives with a packet of biscuits. Domi calls him Gramps, as the girls did when they were little. He calls her 'that Robinson girl', not taking account of the fact that she's been married for twenty-two years and has a completely new surname. He's known her since she was eleven. No wonder he must sometimes get confused. Just whose friend is she? Mine? Hilary's? Frances's? Ellen's?

There are endless comings and goings. The girls pop into Dad's room whenever they are passing to ask if he wants a cup of tea.

Elise and Grandpa are as thick as thieves, ganging up against me. One day I catch Elise rummaging in the larder for biscuits. I know from the cup of tea in her hand and the guilty look on her face that they aren't for her.

'It's almost supper time. Surely Grandpa doesn't want biscuits now, does he?' I remonstrate.

'Grandpa said you'd say that, but I promised him I'd see what I could do. Can't he have just one?' And it's as though she's pleading the case of a baby brother, not a grandpa. I marvel at how seamlessly she has moved from being the little girl who expected her grandpa to look after her to the

181

caring young woman, instinctively wanting to protect this frail, elderly man.

The pride and love I feel for Elise, watching her care for Dad the way he has cared for her, is such a stark reminder of all that went so wrong in the last few months of my marriage.

When he returned from the Caribbean that March, Richard suggested we should up sticks and move there. I was stunned. It was completely unfeasible: the girls were still in school, Dad was up the road and we loved Winchester – or at least Richard had once. So I tried to get that feeling back in him. I arranged diversions in Winchester. We went to the pub, we went out for meals, we went to the cinema. Money was tight, but it would be worth it if he could begin to enjoy life at home again.

I had cautiously started work again. I hadn't worked for twelve months and I was both scared and excited. Before I was ill, writing had become a chore. But after a year away, I missed it desperately and was itching to throw myself into it again. When my first article appeared in the *Daily Mail* in March 2008 – an interview with disability campaigner Henrietta Spink, who had become a friend over the years – I was as thrilled as I'd been when I got my first splash on my first-ever local paper, twenty-five years earlier. I started doing other normal things, too. Tentatively, I began shopping for clothes again. For a whole year, I'd deliberately shut my mind to what I looked like. I hadn't been to the hairdresser. I hadn't bought make-up. I hadn't bought a single item of clothing apart from my special bras. For almost a solid year I'd lived in a couple of Richard's work shirts with trousers. Looking shapeless and sexless let me forget what had happened to my body.

Recovering the first flicker of interest in how I looked was progress, but it was painful. I tried several times to walk into Jigsaw – my favourite shop for well over a decade. Finally, one day, I managed it. I was alone. Fingering the rails of clothes, where once I used to feel totally at home, now all I could see were racks of beautiful, feminine clothes I couldn't wear any more. Too clingy. Too low cut. Cleavage-less, I was undressable. I wanted to – gosh, how I wanted to – try something on, but I couldn't bear to. It was only when, two weeks later, Bridget visited from Edinburgh that I dared venture back. Bridget is a fantastically enthusiastic shopper with a wonderful eye for colour and the ability of a top-flight civil servant – which she is the rest of the time – to weed the wheat from the chaff. Within ten minutes she was ushering me into the changing room with an armful of clothes. Instinctively, she understood what I needed. Clothes that made me feel like the old me but showed off my new short hairstyle, my new lack of curves. Bolstered by Bridget's enthusiasm, I bought a whole new outfit: linen trousers; vest top; silk cardigan. I felt terrific.

But I couldn't shake off a feeling of growing disquiet. As spring turned to summer, we ploughed on regardless, Richard and I leading fairly separate lives. I was arranging trips and treats, organizing meals with friends, but I began to suspect my feelings of emotional separation from Richard had to be more than just a temporary reaction to the stress of coping with my cancer.

Then one day all those walls I'd been so painstakingly building to conceal the truth from myself started to shake. It was July, and Elyssa, the girls' old nanny, who was visiting England from Canada with her new husband, came to stay for a few nights. Elyssa had been working for me when I first met Richard. I'd been giddily drunk on the thrill of being in love; Richard had been bubbling with joy, bursting with bonhomie. Facing the contrast between how we were then and how we were now was stark and unpleasant. In those days we fitted together so perfectly. When we held hands, our skin seemed to merge. His hands were just larger versions of mine – the same tapered fingers, the same pale skin. But now we hardly ever held hands at all. The difference in our relationship could not be plainer.

There was an icy distance that seemed to have solidified between us. It was easier to see the cracks objectively through Elyssa's eyes. So when Richard said he had to rush off during a barbecue to see a client on the other side of town, I noticed his edgy manner. Apparently there was some trouble with a swarm of bees.

It was something about his words. I couldn't put my finger on it, but I knew. Calling over my shoulder that I needed to buy some milk, I got into the car and drove to Karen Taylor's house, my knuckles white on the steering wheel. And I saw what I had dreaded: Richard's car was in the drive. This was not where he had said he was going. I thought of marching up to the front door, but I wasn't wearing make-up and I wasn't wearing my contact lenses – I was enough in control of myself to know that I didn't want to make a scene unless I looked good. So I parked outside and rang Richard's mobile.

There's no need to go into the finer details of how he told me a story that only half made sense, a story I instinctively didn't believe. He of course denied having an affair. I wanted more than anything to believe him.

So that's what I did. Over the next few weeks I carried on pretending that nothing was wrong – like a demented party planner on the *Titanic*, initiating games of pass the parcel and musical chairs while the ship sinks below the surface. I decided to throw a party to celebrate my fiftieth birthday that September. It would also be an opportunity to bring together all the disparate friends who'd been my backbone when I was ill.

I hurled myself into the fun of party organizing. With the girls, I pored over the guest list. Elise helped with choosing and writing the invitations. But when the day came, it was hard even for me, struggling to keep a toehold in my perennially cheerful little cocoon, to ignore how uncomfortable things had become with Richard.

The party was a modest affair. Drinks in the garden, platters of Marks and Spencer food laid out in the kitchen.

Almost everyone who mattered to me was there, plus assorted husbands and children: my nieces, Frances and Sibylla; Helen, Debs, Julie, Bridget, Cherry and Rosalind – my gang of girlfriends from university; Dominique, my oldest schoolfriend; workmates Amanda, Ingrid and Madeleine; pregnancy pals Sally and Fiona who'd bonded with me through the shared humiliation of ante-natal classes; Anne, my chemo chum; and Angela my friend from journalism college. Elise's godmother, Anne, had flown in from Northern Ireland for the weekend. There were local friends, too: Tracey and Martin and Fran and Chris who'd helped shield the girls from the worst of my illness. Simon had flown down from Edinburgh, Andy had come from Brighton. And, of course, Dad was there, delighted to help celebrate, delighted to be made a fuss of by my friends. I felt enveloped by affection.

But Richard wasn't there. He might have been physically present, but the man I loved had disappeared. I longed for us to hug and be able to show our friends how happy we were, but I knew deep down that we weren't. The only times Richard seemed happy were when he was windsurfing or had just come back from the Caribbean.

That day, as I tried to put thoughts of our unsettled relationship aside, something happened to bring it home again. During a conversation with one of my closest friends, she got very serious and commented on our apparent estrangement. She asked me whether something had happened. I was stunned and unprepared to hear someone acknowledge the gulf between us. I told her she was wrong, that we were fine, but I didn't believe myself when I said it. My thoughts went to his odd behaviour and my previous suspicions of him having an affair. I wasn't imagining it. Now I knew that others had noticed, too. I knew I had to talk to Richard.

The rest of the party was painful and exhausting for me. I thought of Richard's incredible support throughout my illness and couldn't believe he would ever be unfaithful, but I kept coming back to the conversation with my friend. That night, I asked him again whether he was having an affair. Once again he denied it and we didn't discuss it further. The gulf between us seemed to grow with every minute we avoided the topic.

The next day was my actual birthday. I woke at 6.30 a.m. to the sound of the letterbox snapping shut. Dad had walked around with a card for me. Inside was a cheque for £500. I was so touched, I wanted to rush up the road after him in my pyjamas and hug him. There was no gift from Richard, but he had booked a table for us at the Black Rat, the same Michelin-starred restaurant where we had celebrated our tenth wedding anniversary the previous year. However, after the emotional upheaval of my birthday party, and the painful conversations with my friend and with Richard, I asked him to cancel. Richard was upset, but all I felt was terrible dread. I was too exhausted and too frightened about what was going on to sit face to face with him through a lavish meal. I knew we couldn't get through an entire evening without talking about the one topic we were avoiding.

And then something completely unexpected happened. I had another cancer scare. It was two weeks after my party. My GP had referred me to the hospital because, ever since I had finished my chemotherapy, I had been experiencing very heavy periods. She thought it could be a side-effect of the Tamoxifen I was taking, but she wanted to be sure. I went in for a consultation, expecting a brief check-up. Instead, after examining me, the consultant asked me to come in the following day for an operation.

'There's something on your right ovary,' he said. 'We need to know what it is.'

'You mean it could be cancerous?' I asked, my bottom lip quivering.

'Well, we need to rule that out,' he said tactfully.

I had dared to begin to believe that the cancer was behind me. I was in such shock, I could barely walk out of the room, let alone drive home. I rang Richard and, as he bounced into the waiting room, I felt so grateful that he was there for me. All the familiar feelings came flooding back. My love for him. My need of him. My belief in him. I was going to fight to make this marriage work. Later that night, I hugged him in bed, grateful for the warmth of his body.

We sat up late into the night talking about things. And I realized that it was a long, long time since we'd properly talked.

Richard drove me back to hospital the following morning. He kissed me goodbye as I was led off to my bed. Mercifully, it seemed like minutes before I was coming to again. The consultant was beside my bed. 'It's all done.' He smiled. 'It was a simple polyp, which we've removed.'

'So no cancer?' I asked.

'No – it was all beautifully clear,' he said.

Relief flooded through me. But, more than the relief, I felt a huge surge of energy, like a racing engine roaring into full throttle. I could move mountains. I could part seas. I could face the truth. I just needed one more push.

I didn't have to wait long. A friend told me that Richard had mentioned he planned to spend the winter working in the Caribbean. This was the first I had heard of it. Now there was absolutely no denying that he was putting Karen before me. I was finally ready for a confrontation.

One of Dad's expressions popped into my head: 'To thine own self be true.' It's Polonius's advice to his son in *Hamlet*. Dad had written it in my autograph book decades ago. I remembered how Dad has always had such innate self-belief. Though he rose from the humblest origins, he has never been in awe of anyone, and he brought me up to feel the same. Arriving at Oxford fresh from my very ordinary comprehensive school may have been daunting, but never, for one second, did I think I wasn't good enough to be there. Dad made sure of that. He and Mum also drummed into all of us that we should follow our consciences. Now Dad's words propelled me on.

I waited for Richard to get home. I waited for him to have a bath and get changed. I waited for the girls to go out for the evening. I waited for Richard to pour himself a glass of wine – and then I knew I didn't need to wait any longer.

As he settled himself in front of his laptop and I sat on the sofa, I said: 'I know you are having an affair and you have to tell me the truth.'

This time he didn't deny it.

NINE

HOLD YOUR HEAD UP HIGH

To cut a long and painful story short, over the course of that evening I learned the full facts of Richard's affair, in the forensic detail I demanded. It felt as though knowing everything would make up for knowing nothing for so long. I finally heard him admit that he'd been having an affair with Karen Taylor and it had been going on a very long time.

I was sick with shock, but there was also a sense of relief. I'd been driving myself mad for so long. Now everything clicked into place. All the trips to the Caribbean and the windsurfing, the distance between us and the terrible loneliness and unhappiness I felt suddenly made total sense.

Richard was upset and remorseful, he had persuasive excuses – but I finally knew for certain that we weren't on the same side any more. At that instant, self-preservation kicked in. Now I had the truth and the only thing that mattered was doing what was best for me and the girls. And that meant getting Richard out of the house. I knew that, with him around, I wouldn't be able to think straight. I'm my father's daughter, all right: it felt like there wasn't a moment to lose.

I wanted him gone, but exhausted from the confrontation, we spent that night in the same bed. I knew it was for the last time. Perhaps a tiny bit of him suspected it was, too.

Richard had agreed to go and spend a week with his mother to give me time and space to think. Watching him dress in the morning, I knew I would never see him naked again. Eleven years of mornings just like this. Our old life had been swept away, but we still had to go through the motions of being married for another few hours. That Saturday morning I was helping organize a lecture followed by a buffet lunch in Winchester for fellow graduates of my Oxford college. Richard came with me to pick up the food and drove me there.

At the church hall, Richard helped me unload the shopping bags. When he tried to kiss me goodbye, I pushed him away. But then I ran after him. I couldn't bear this to be the last thing he remembered of our marriage.

'We've been together a long time,' I said, as I leant into the car window to kiss him goodbye. 'Drive safely.'

He was crying. 'Darling, I'm so, so sorry.'

The morning passed in a total blur. I was grateful to be preoccupied. My fixed smile only wavered at the end, when we were clearing up. 'There's lots of food left over. Take it home for Richard and the girls,' someone said. My heart lurched. How could I start to explain what had happened when I didn't really believe it myself? So I trudged home with a carrier bag full of sausage rolls, pork pies and sand-wiches for a husband who didn't live with me any more. This was going to be so much harder than I dared contem-plate. A marriage to unpick. A family to be prised apart. A home to be broken up. Friends and relatives to be told. Habits to be broken.

Back home, I couldn't keep up the front any longer. I put on a Dusty Springfield CD at full blast then sat in the arm-chair in front of the Aga and howled. I had wanted to hide my despair from the girls but I knew I couldn't conceal what had happened. They came bursting into the kitchen and I mustered the best story I could find.

'Richard and I have had a row. He's gone to stay with Grandma while we try and sort things out, but I'm not sure whether we can stay married. We're both so unhappy,' I said.

I hadn't wanted to tell them about his affair at first. I thought they would condemn him and I wanted to leave them with some respect for him. I owed him that. But it was all too late. They were more prepared for the news than I had been. While I had been hiding from the truth, they had noticed the huge distance between us and Richard's growing unhappiness. They quizzed me and I couldn't lie. I told them everything.

I became obsessed with finding evidence. I needed evi-dence – to torture myself, if nothing else. Like a wild dervish, I ransacked Richard's drawers, hunting for clues, which were plentiful and easy to find. I couldn't believe I'd been so blind. We'd always had separate bank accounts, so, until now, I'd never really known how he'd spent his money. Now I could see.

As that terrible evening raged on, any lingering scrap of desire to try and save the marriage vanished. I'd been so like my mum, obstinately blind to the possibility of being lied to. Dad has always been much more worldly-wise, more astute about what makes people tick. But Mum's gullibility was a blindspot. She couldn't accept that there are people who might lie routinely – particularly sensible, intelligent people. Particularly anyone in a close relationship. And, in all the years I've been away from her, all the people I've interviewed, all the court cases I've sat through, I still find it hard to be suspicious. If someone tells me something – however outrageous – I'm inclined to believe they are telling me the truth.

The fury I felt now was partly at my own stupidity. I replayed years of memories in my mind, searching for clues I should have picked up on, peculiar incidents, things said that instinctively didn't add up but I'd never questioned. I was shaking with shock when finally I went to bed. I couldn't sleep that night, nor the next. Everything in the room reminded me of Richard. Every segment of our conversations played over and over again in my head like a relentless horror movie, torturing me – but still I found it almost impossible to believe that it had really happened. I sobbed silently into my pillow that night so that the girls wouldn't hear and worry.

I barely had the energy to get dressed. And I couldn't be

bothered to cook. We ate reheated spaghetti bolognaise for four nights on the trot. All the minutiae of normal life carried a hideous reminder that Richard had gone. I didn't know what to do with his dirty clothes. Did I wash them? Did I leave them to fester? There's no textbook to tell you what to do with a load of boxer shorts in your laundry basket when the husband they belong to has gone.

Richard was coming back to Winchester at the weekend, and I needed to feel calm before I saw him again. In the meantime, I decided to write him a letter. I wanted him to know that the marriage was over.

'I'm sorry that things have ended this way,' I began.

I loved you so much and wanted so badly for you to be happy that I trusted you beyond the bounds of common sense. I'm sure you can understand that I feel revolted, betrayed and terribly wounded by your behaviour. I feel very angry that you allowed the girls to suffer under the shadow of this for so long. They trusted you and deserved so much better. But, most of all, I feel immense sorrow. It's such a waste.

I posted it to his mother's and, once I'd sent it, I felt much better.

I had dreaded telling Dad what had happened. I knew he would be shocked. He had always liked Richard. And Richard had been a faultless son-in-law – kind, solicitous, dutiful. It was one of the things I loved about him. Something I would always remind myself of when I got irritated with him. He'd never demurred when I suggested taking Dad on holiday with us and went out of his way to make him feel welcome. We'd all been to Madrid and France together. In March 2005, we'd celebrated Dad's ninetieth birthday in Normandy. Dad had always wanted to see the Bayeux Tapestry. While we were there – more at our behest than his – we visited Arromanches, the site of the D-Day Landings. In the museum, Dad was treated like a hero. He was granted free entry. American tourists sidled over to ask, in awed tones, if he had fought there. They wanted their photos taken with Dad – a genuine gold-plated D-Day survivor. Dad was bemused by the attention but smiled gamely for the cameras, shoulders thrown back in proper military fashion. He loved France. He loved having breakfast in the snug little hotel restaurant and asking Madame for '*du lait*' with his coffee. It was a phrase he'd picked up in 1944 and never had the occasion to use since. Now, sixty years later, it tripped off his tongue.

I intended to break the news gently to Dad. But it came rushing out.

'Daddy, I've asked Richard to leave. I can't live with him any more,' I began.

Dad was flummoxed. 'I know you can be hot-tempered. What is it? Have you had a squabble?' he asked anxiously.

'It's worse than that, Dad. He's been having an affair

with a woman he works for. I love him – we've been through so much together – but I'll never forgive him.'

'Tessa, love, are you sure?'

'Absolutely, Dad. It would be different if it had been just a fling. But it wasn't. The affair's been going on a long time. He's hurt me and the girls so much for so long that I can't forgive him. And even if I could, I'd never trust him or respect him again. It's over,' I sobbed.

Dad took his big white handkerchief out of his cardigan pocket and started dabbing gently at my face, which made me cry even more. He was visibly shocked and he took a long time to say anything. When he did speak, it wasn't what I was expecting. I thought he might try and defend Richard, try and persuade me to take him back because he was worried how I would cope alone. But as far as Dad was concerned, Richard had crossed the Rubicon. He had humiliated me and, in his book, that was intolerable. And, as for worrying whether I could cope, it didn't even enter his head.

'Come now, my sweet,' he said finally. 'I know it's going to be hard, but if Richard's treated you like this, you're right to send him packing. You'd end up losing respect for yourself if you stayed with him. I know Mum would agree. She'd never allow any man to treat her badly, me included, and you mustn't either. I always regarded Mum as more than my equal and that's how every woman should be treated by her husband. You deserve so much better.'

And I remembered how my dear old, totally undomesticated dad would never let Mum wash a kitchen floor or clean a bathroom their entire married life because he thought it was demeaning.

I also remembered how the month before Hilary was going to get married, Brian announced that he had found a flat for them to rent in London. Hilary, twenty-one, was living at home in the run-up to the wedding, so Mum and Dad drove her over to look at it. It was in Islington. But this was 1968 and Islington was not posh. And this flat was particularly rank. It was one dingy, damp room with a primus stove in the corner. The bathroom was down the corridor and it was shared with three other families.

Dad took Brian to one side. 'If you think you are going to marry my daughter and bring her to live here, you are very much mistaken,' he said sternly.

Brian, who was used to getting his own way, tried to argue. 'It's all I can afford.'

'In that case, you are going to have to wait until you can afford something better,' said Dad. 'I won't be giving my daughter away to come and live in this hovel. She deserves much better and I'm disappointed you don't realize it.'

Brian was quietly seething. Hilary was furious. But, as Dad got back in the car and prepared to leave, it was obvious who was going to win.

A few weeks later, Brian found a flat in Golders Green with an inside toilet and a garden. Dad felt totally vindicated. If Brian was still angry, he never let on, and Dad, careful not to humiliate him any further, never mentioned it again.

I'd known that Dad would support me, whatever I decided to do. But it was his faith in me that I needed. Over and over again in the next few weeks the same questions would go round in my mind: 'How could Richard treat me so badly? Why did I let him?' And every time, Dad's words would bolster me: 'You are strong. You deserve so much better.'

Dad has helped raise six girls – my sister Hilary and me, her daughters and mine – and he's given us an invaluable gift: self-belief. Dad firmly believes that women are the stronger sex. When Mum trained to be a teacher aged almost fifty, after twenty-two years at home bringing up children, Dad was inordinately proud of her. He didn't even demur when the first thing she did was rush off and open her own personal bank account, for the sheer thrill of having financial independence. 'She told the cashier: "I want my own account. He's not getting his hands on my lolly",' laughs Dad indulgently when he tells the story. 'You know, those years when Mum was teaching were among the happiest of our marriage. She was desperate for a career and loved the idea of helping kids and I backed her all the way. She was far too talented and intelligent to stay at home, twiddling her thumbs.'

Dad's very modern attitude is particularly striking as he came from a generation in which women didn't work and his poor mother was treated like a skivvy by her husband.

Or perhaps that's the key. Dad adored his mum. He sent her money from his wages every week; he took her on holiday to the seaside every summer. He was heartbroken when she died in 1944 just before he married Mum. She was barely into her fifties, worn out by childbirth and hardship. Dad blamed his father and never forgave him, refusing even to go to his funeral.

'That bully of a man gave my mother a hellish life,' he says. 'He complained about every meal he ever ate. He thought it was clever because it would keep my poor mum on her toes. But the truth is that he did it because he was weak. If you are strong, you don't throw your weight around.'

Even so, after Richard left, I felt weaker than I ever had. His deception struck at the very heart of who I was, in a way even cancer hadn't managed to do. It ate away at the person I had always believed myself to be – intelligent, capable, loveable. Because the truth is that no sensible woman should allow her husband to have an affair over several years. Yet I had. Why had I allowed this to happen to me? Why had I ignored the signs for so long? What was wrong with me?

I still felt weak and pathetic when Dad moved in. If I'm honest, that was probably part of the reason for agreeing to have him live with me in the first place. I wanted to prove to myself that I was strong enough to cope. And so the satisfaction of those early days was immense. Of all the moments

I'm proudest of in my life, the moment I walked with Dad into his new room for the first time, is one of the very, very best . . . followed by the moment the next day when he woke and saw Elise sitting beside him.

'What on earth are you doing here, love? Shouldn't you be at home?' he asked.

'But Grandpa, this is my home,' she said. And I knew then that he felt totally comfortable and so much at home that he'd imagined he actually was back in his own little apartment.

We visit Mum's grave every so often. Dad used to go at least once a month to check that the granite gravestone was free of moss, the grass cut. Now, it's quite a performance. I have to push Dad in his wheelchair over the uneven ground, in between the gravestones. Last time we went, as I knelt beside Dad on the damp grass and took his hand, I suddenly remembered Mum's words to me before she died.

'Will you look after Daddy for me?'

It had seemed like a curse. I wasn't ready to do it and I was so relieved that, far from needing to be looked after, Dad was the one doing all the caring and supporting. But now here I am, sixteen years later. And it's working. And that makes me feel better about myself than I have in a long time.

As we leave, Dad jokes: 'I always used to come here to get my instructions from Mum.'

'Ah, but Dad, you don't need to any more. They're all being channelled through me!'

Dad pulls a face. 'Ooh, if it's not one bossy woman, it's another,' he says. And I want to hug him for loving me, for helping make me feel strong and capable again, and for coming to live with me at the exact moment when I needed him most.

TEN

LET THE PAST GO

I was so decisive about ending my marriage that you might think that everything that followed was plain sailing. But that would be totally and completely wrong. In fact, the fallout drove me to the edge of a nervous breakdown. Most of the time in that first week, while Richard was with his mother, I was convinced that I had done the right thing. My friends rallied round.

They divided into different camps. Some were stunned by the news. Others found that it made everything fall into place. They all offered possible motivations; some even felt sorry for him, saying it must have been his own failings, his insecurities that drove him to act like this

There were moments over the weeks that followed when my resolve began to crumble. Had some of it been my fault? I'd been so focused on my career; perhaps I had neglected him, perhaps I had forced him into Karen Taylor's arms. Should I at least consider giving him a second chance?

Any such shred of doubt was gone after weeks of

reconciliatory meetings, discussions and even counselling with Richard, when promises were made and broken and things said that didn't add up. He said he wanted to come back. He said he loved me, but would he really give up Karen Taylor? I just felt even more confused and demented. Karen Taylor. I had no idea who she was. I had to know what she looked like. I had to let her know how I felt.

Dad understood what I was going through. 'Leave it alone, love. You won't achieve anything by confronting her. It's a part of your life that's over and you have to let it go. You'll never make her understand how you feel. She doesn't want to know.'

I should have listened. After all, Dad had spent his entire married life trying to get Mum to understand that there are times when you have to live and let live. One of the things that endeared Mum to my father but which also drove him wild with frustration at times was that she was so damned forthright. She believed in open dialogue at all times, in all situations.

Dad often grumbled: 'You would argue with the flaming Pope.'

'Of course I would – if I thought he was wrong,' Mum, a devout Catholic, would answer defiantly.

If she saw something she disapproved of, she felt honour bound to speak up. If she saw an injustice, she felt obliged to point it out; and if she felt misunderstood, she could not rest until she had explained herself. She called it 'getting her point across'. It might be unpleasant, it might be painful, but, in Mum's eyes, if you didn't have things out with people or try and get to the bottom of things, you were being cowardly.

Her favourite expression was: 'I must just say . . . '

We would tease her 'Mum, you really don't need to.' But she felt she did.

When I was planning to marry my first husband, Mum took it upon herself to try and stop the marriage. She was right, as it turned out.

'You don't really love him, I know you don't,' she said. Did I listen? Of course not. I was thirty-two and convinced that I knew best. I was furious, particularly when she sent me a letter saying exactly the same thing. Dad understood that she was never going to make me agree, but Mum wouldn't give up.

A week before the wedding, I asked her what she would be wearing.

There was a long pause. 'I thought I'd wait and see,' she said.

'What, see if I'm going to get married?'

'Well, yes, since you ask.'

But, when my marriage ended just four years later, did Mum say: 'I told you so?' Not at all. The flip-side of Mum's often hugely inconvenient mania for truth and openness was that she never held a grudge.

Years later, long after Mum died, my friend Helen told me that Mum had sought her out at the wedding reception. Helen was nursing her two-week-old baby when Mum appeared. She sat down in the chair next to her and took Helen's hand. She was almost in tears as she said: 'You will look after Tessa, won't you?'

'Of course,' said Helen, taken aback.

'And we will have to be standing by her when this all goes wrong.'

'It was a pact,' Helen recalls. 'I'd always been a little in awe of your mum, but that day I saw how much she loved you and I would have done anything to help.'

I knew from a few stray remarks that Dad had never liked my first husband either, but he was much better than Mum at masking it.

Although I tried to hide my anguish from Dad, he could see I was in turmoil during this awful time with Richard. Having lived with Mum for over fifty years, he sensed what was driving me.

'Sweet, you can't make other people do your bidding. If Richard's not man enough to behave well, you can't make him. And as for the woman he's taken up with – well, she's not worth wasting a second's thought on. For your own peace of mind, let it go.'

He was right, of course, but a mixture of Mum's mania for the truth and Dad's impetuosity propelled me on. The emotional storm raging inside me was so cataclysmic that I didn't think I could breathe another day if I didn't find a way of externalizing it. I had to confront Karen Taylor. I had to understand what was going on. And so, one afternoon in early December, I drove to her house. And I thought of the first time I had been there, when I had strolled up to the door with one of Richard's flyers in my hand. The devoted little wife, leafleting to help her husband's business. How could I possibly have guessed what it would lead to?

Now, five years later, as I strode purposefully up the drive, I didn't know what I was going to find, and, underneath the air of confidence, I was petrified. I took a deep breath and rang the doorbell. Richard was there. He answered the door, vacuum cleaner in hand, his welcoming smile turning into glassy-eyed shock.

'Oh, hi,' he stuttered. 'This is a surprise. No one's in, I'm afraid,'

'But you are,' I replied, firmly stepping forward as he moved back to let me in. Even if I couldn't meet her, I might at last discover who she was and what was really going on between them. That might give me some peace.

I felt immensely powerful and icily calm as I marched through the hallway and straight up the stairs. Too stunned to protest, Richard led me around. I marched from room to room until I found myself in her bedroom. Anger coursed through me and I was desperate to know what she looked like. There were photos on her dressing table. Without thinking straight, I took one and stuffed it into my handbag.

Now I would know what she looked like. And now she'd know that I had been in her bedroom and that Richard had let me. She'd humiliated me for years. Now I'd done the same to her. It went a tiny way to even the score. There was no more to see. I marched triumphantly downstairs and out of the house.

Back home, I was on a high, giddy with the thrill of wresting control at last, of laying to rest all those clanking ghosts of Karen Taylor. Then I looked at the photo I'd taken from her bedroom and I saw, with a sense of shock, that it was a young girl, not Karen – it had been taken too recently to be her. She must be a relative, a close relative.

For a second, I felt a quiver of demonic delight. This woman had trampled all over my marriage. Now I'd got something she treasured. But, as I looked more closely at the photo, I felt sick with myself, recognizing that this girl must matter to her. I loathed Karen Taylor, but I knew that I had to give the photo back to her. I could have posted it, but I still needed to see her, to know what she looked like – and I still hoped she would apologize. After a few days, I picked the photo up and drove to her house again.

Adrenaline was pumping as I walked up to the door. I rang twice before the door was finally opened. And there – at last – was Karen Taylor. I took in all that I saw in an instant and I was relieved, because I wasn't impressed.

The next few moments were not my finest, nor were they likely hers. We snarled and drawled at each other, our tones reeking with bitterness and contempt. There was no apology from her, far from it; in fact she closed the door in my face. And that is when I completely lost it. Red-hot fury erupted inside my gut like molten lava.

I was still holding the envelope with the photo in it. I shoved it through the letter box. I turned to go and then I thought: 'How dare she slam the door in my face?' I hammered as hard as I could on the glass panel in her front door. I hoped that if I could make a loud enough noise, expend enough of the adrenaline coursing inside me, I could exorcize some of the rage. What I hadn't accounted for was that my hand would go straight through the glass. Shards scattered on to the doormat. In the empty space I could see Karen Taylor jumping back in alarm, and, as I looked at my hand, I could see huge globules of blood.

A three-inch-long crescent-shaped cut ran along the heel of my hand and my knuckles were ripped. I looked as though I'd wandered off the set of a slasher movie. Blood was spurting like water from a drinking fountain. I was beginning to feel faint. In the car, I grappled in my handbag for a couple of tissues and wrapped them tightly around my hand and then I drove as fast as I could to the Accident and Emergency department, blood splattering on to the steering wheel.

My hand now throbbing in pain, I looked in such dire straits that the receptionist ushered me straight in to see a doctor. After one look at my hand, it was obvious that I was going to need a lot of stitches.

I wasn't prepared when the nurse asked for my next of kin. Without thinking, I gave her Richard's name.

'We'll contact your husband. You need someone with you,' she said.

I didn't have the words to explain that he wasn't really

my husband any more and that it was his fault that this had happened. Meekly, I reeled off his mobile phone number.

Richard arrived just as the doctor began to stitch up my hand. He looked even paler than I did when he saw all the blood. He sat down and took my left hand while the doctor worked on my right.

'Poor you,' he said. 'Just try and stay calm.'

I squeezed his soft, familiar hand, as pain radiated through my whole body. The last time I had held his hand like this in a hospital room was when chemotherapy drugs were being pumped into me. Now here we were, back in the same hospital barely a year later because I'd smashed my hand through his girlfriend's glass door. It seemed utterly unbelievable.

As the curtains around my bed swished open and closed with the nurses coming and going, I dimly became aware that a policeman was standing outside in the corridor. At first I thought he must be guarding a prisoner. But every time the curtains opened, he was there, looking at me. And suddenly I understood. I was the prisoner. He was making sure that I didn't shin up over the back wall of the hospital, scattering my dressings behind me. And, as I thought about it further, I realized that Karen Taylor must have reported me to the police for breaking the pane of glass. And was it Richard, who was sitting beside me holding my hand, who had told them where I was? It was possible that Karen had guessed I'd go to the nearest hospital. But I was beyond giving Richard the benefit of the doubt.

At that moment, the last tiny drop of love dripped away. I didn't say another word to Richard in the two hours it took to stitch up my hand. The doctor looked helpless as the policeman accompanied me outside, Richard trailing behind looking hangdog.

As ambulances swished by, the policeman arrested me on suspicion of criminal damage. He read me my rights. I'd seen it hundreds of times on TV – although I'm not sure I'd ever seen it in a hospital car park. Then he led me to his panda car. I was not allowed to call the girls, so I reluctantly accepted Richard's offer to do it instead. I got in the police car and left Richard standing on the kerb.

At the police station, after fingerprinting, having my mouth swabbed for DNA samples and handing over my scarf and handbag, I was allowed one phone call – to a duty solicitor. I was given a number and pointed to a phone hanging on the wall beside the cells. The solicitor was very sweet and reassuring. On the downside, her office was an hour's drive away. 'I'll get to you as quickly as I can and hopefully we'll get you out tonight,' she said.

Hopefully? I didn't really like the sound of that. But I had much more immediate worries. I had to beg another phone call.

'I know this may sound trivial, but my daughter is due at the dentist in thirty minutes. She's in the middle of really expensive private treatment and I need to cancel, otherwise I might never be forgiven,' I begged.

The custody officer smiled understandingly. 'Of course,

love. I know what these dentists can be like. I'll make the phone call for you. And, don't worry, I won't say where you are.' That was a relief. I didn't like to think about Ellen left with a brace for life because I'd been banged up in a police cell.

Meanwhile, his deputy led me off to my cell. He had a big tummy, bushy eyebrows and a kindly smile.

'I bet you'd fancy a nice hot cup of tea?'

I perked up instantly. I'd had nothing to eat or drink since breakfast, seven hours ago. And, on top of the shock, the blood loss and the excitement of a drive in a police car, I was feeling decidedly peculiar.

'Nice and milky?'

'Yes, please. Any chance of a biscuit?'

He smiled proudly. 'We can do better than that. What do you fancy? Cheese toastie? Burger and chips? All-day breakfast? Tuna pasta bake?'

'Tuna pasta bake?'

'Always very popular.'

'Yes, please.'

Unlocking the door, he showed me around my new cell, pointing out the facilities with all the eagerness of a hotel bellboy. Unfortunately, the tour didn't take long because there was only a metal bench and a toilet. It didn't have a door and there wasn't a proper seat. But at least the cell was all mine. I wouldn't say that I'd spent my entire life wondering what a cell looked like from the inside, but it was certainly satisfying to find out at last.

'So you're going to be all right then?' he asked solicitously as he prepared to lock me in.

'I don't suppose you've got any magazines?'

He looked doubtful. 'I'll see what I can find. Back in a sec.'

Fifteen minutes later he was back with a huge mug of tea, a gargantuan tuna bake in a polystyrene carton, and copies of *Motorcycle Monthly* and *Angling Times*. I'd have preferred *Marie Claire* or *Cosmo*, but what the hell. And as I settled back on my metal bench and sipped my tea, I felt at peace for the first time in seven and a half weeks. My life as Richard's wife was over. My fury with Karen Taylor was spent. What I did was impulsive but I didn't regret it at all. I was no longer angry. I didn't care whether they felt sorry for what they had done or not. I didn't care a damn for either of them. It had been worth all the pain, all the drama. I felt powerful for the first time in ages. I was free.

It was 6.30 p.m. when the solicitor finally arrived. She didn't look much older than my girls, and I felt sorry that she was about to get such a brutal education in the breakdown of a marriage. I told her the whole story from the beginning. She blanched.

'Gosh. Well, we definitely need to get you home. While you've been in here, a policeman has been taking a statement from Mrs Taylor. Once he's read that, he'll want to hear your version of events. You simply tell him exactly what you've told me and you'll go home.'

My solicitor sat beside me in the interview room while the duty officer ceremoniously flicked on his tape recorder and asked me to recount exactly what had happened. The affair. The marriage breakdown. The photo. The confrontation on the doorstep. It all seemed a very, very long time ago.

When I finished, he thanked me, clicked off the machine and disappeared out of the room. He was soon back with a sheaf of papers.

'If you are prepared to accept a caution, I think we can have this all wrapped up.'

'A caution?'

The solicitor interjected: 'It's a sort of police warning. It's for someone who's never been in trouble before and has committed a minor offence – in this case, criminal damage.'

'Criminal damage?'

'It sounds worse than it is. It's like if someone decides to play football in the middle of the street. They ought to realize that they might break a window. And if they do, it's called criminal damage,' she explained.

I didn't see any benefit in pointing out the other side of the story: that if someone chooses to have an affair, they ought to realize there might be collateral damage. Besides, I did understand that you can't have aggrieved wives the length and breadth of Britain marching around to other women's homes and smashing glass door panels just for the hell of it. Where would it all end?

The officer carefully typed out my offence and, resignedly,

I signed at the bottom. 'The defendant has attended an address and through vigorous knocking at the door caused a pane of glass to break which she accepts was reckless and as a direct result of her actions.' I would probably have phrased it a little more emotively myself, but it was a decent enough epitaph on my marriage.

It was 8 p.m. when I was released. My car was still in the hospital car park, so I walked home. The fresh air did me good. The girls took one look at my hand and freaked out.

'Richard told us you'd had an accident. What happened?' said Ellen.

They were shocked. But, as far as they were concerned, they were glad that I'd done what I felt I needed to do, no matter how dramatic the consequences.

I slept better that night than I had in months. The first thing I found when I woke up the next morning was that I felt totally calm. It was such a novel emotion, I'd almost forgotten what it felt like. I decided to celebrate by taking the girls Christmas shopping. I couldn't drive. So the girls and I went to Southampton by train. During the day, I got a text from Richard. I did what I should have done six weeks earlier. I sent him a text: 'Please don't contact me again.'

It had taken me a very, very long time, but finally I had done what Dad had advised me to do right at the start. I had washed my hands of him – and her. They would never be able to hurt me again.

ELEVEN

IGNORANCE IS BLISSFUL

I never told Dad about what happened the day I met Karen Taylor and how I had cut my hand. In fact, I never even told him her name. I knew he would find it too upsetting if he had to put a name to this 'other woman' – the one he chose never to think about. In fact, he went out of his way to behave as though Richard had never been part of our lives. He discreetly removed the wedding photos from his cabinet and never talked about him again.

When he noticed the bandage, I glossed over it as a minor accident and he didn't ask any more questions. Instead, he stalwartly ignored the fact that for two weeks I sported a huge white bandage on my hand.

'You look as though you've been in the wars, love, but as long as you are OK now,' he said. And that's how he left it.

Having Dad there, a beacon of sense acting as though everything were normal in the midst of all the madness, was the best possible help. But, the truth is that, even bolstered by Dad's unquestioning love and support, I was a mess.

After Richard left, I lost over a stone. I was so thin that one morning I put on a skirt and it fell straight to the floor. Looking in the mirror, I reminded myself of when I was ill – huge bug eyes, scrawny frame, jutting hip bones. However much I ate – giant bowls of soup, slabs of chocolate cake, double helpings of pudding – I couldn't seem to shift above eight stone. I slathered butter and mayonnaise on everything. At lunch with girlfriends, they would order Caesar salad (light on the dressing) and pick at crumbs of bread while I troughed my way through a plateful of chicken pie with mashed potato followed by bread-and-butter pudding, washed down with a milky café latte. I was terrified that my dramatic weight loss was a sign that the cancer had come back. One day, in desperation, I went to Holland and Barrett. I scoured the shelves looking for weight-gain supplements. When I couldn't find any, I walked up to the counter for assistance.

'Look at me. I'm so thin,' I said. 'I need something to help me put on weight – some sort of bulking-up stuff.'

The young girl behind the counter seemed surprisingly disinclined to assist. 'I don't really know what to say,' she said, shrugging.

'Surely you can recommend something . . . anything,' I begged. 'Just show me where to look.'

She sighed pointedly. Then, very slowly, she eased herself from behind the counter and it was only then that I saw she was the size of a sumo wrestler. And, as she waddled across the floor, it was all she could do to contain her fury with me.

I was so mortified I felt like bursting into tears. But then that was nothing unusual. I was doing an awful lot of crying.

The slightest thing would set me off. Putting the bins out, which had always been Richard's job. Putting 'divorced' on official forms to describe my about-to-be marital status. Putting Richard's clothes, his tin full of spare suit buttons and his teddy bear into black bin liners and hiding them somewhere I wouldn't have to see them every day. Receiving Christmas cards addressed to Richard and Tessa from the people I still hadn't told. Finding the bottle of home-made sloe gin we'd made together aeons ago carefully labelled in Richard's neat handwriting. Being introduced to strangers who wanted to know what my husband did for a living, when all I wanted was to sneer: 'You mean, apart from sleeping with his client base?' And worst – by far the worst – of all was Christmas. My first Christmas in eleven years not waking up next to Richard, not wrapping the presents, not making the mince pies, not cooking the turkey, not listening to Phil Spector with him.

Funnily enough, the only person I didn't cry in front of was Dad. It wasn't out of a noble desire not to hurt him. When I was with Dad, I felt safe. He never had a long face. He never asked me how I was or did any of those things that most people do to show compassion, which often just end up making you feel much worse. He never asked how I was bearing up, whether I was eating enough or sleeping properly. He did what he always did – what he'd done when I was ill – and acted as though nothing out of the ordinary had happened and that I would be absolutely fine.

Even tiny moments of joy barely made a dent in my armour of misery. In late January, Ellen got the offer of a place at the Courtauld Institute of Art. She was ecstatic. So was I . . . briefly. But all too soon I was plagued with worries: 'What if she didn't get the grades? What if it all fell through?' All the frantic optimism I'd acquired when my treatment finished had evaporated. I found it hard to imagine that anything was ever going to go right again.

In short, I was in danger of completely and comprehensively cracking up. I recognized the feelings from when I was ill. And I was terrified. This time, I didn't have Richard to help heave me out of the morass. I would have to do it myself and I didn't know if I had the stamina. There were days, whole weeks in fact, when all I wanted was for somebody to knock me on the head and let me rest for six months. Perhaps when I came to, I might feel strong enough to cope. But now I really didn't.

I must admit I never even tried to discuss this with Dad. He's of the old school that believes that depression is self-indulgent and that blaming stress for anything is just a way of trying to avoid facing up to things.

One day in January, my friend Amanda rang. I said: 'Hello,' and then I started crying and I couldn't stop. She was alarmed.

'I want you to ring the doctor and make an appointment

right now. And then I want you to ring me back and tell me that you've done it,' she said.

So I did. Two hours later, I was sitting beside my doctor as she offered me tissues. Maybe I'd stopped crying in the interim, but I'm not sure. She asked if I felt suicidal. I surprised myself by whispering: 'I don't know. All I know is that I don't want to have this pain any longer.'

I explained what had happened and how I couldn't see a way out.

'I'm frightened the stress is going to bring the cancer back,' I sobbed.

'I don't believe that's going to happen,' she said. 'But I think you might need something to tide you over the next few months.'

She prescribed me an anti-depressant called citalopram. I didn't demur. I wanted something, anything, to take away the pain in my head. And that night – for the first time in three months – I had a totally uninterrupted night of sleep. I could feel my heart slow, my body relax, the anxiety ebb away. Within ten days I was beginning to feel almost normal again.

I decided to go back to counselling. I needed somebody who wasn't one of my long-suffering friends to listen to me and help me make sense of what had happened. So every Thursday morning for six weeks from late January through to March, I had an hour's session with Mandy, the very same counsellor Richard and I had seen. Together we dissected all the things that had gone wrong with my marriage and why. I cried. Mandy offered tissues. And when whole days went by in which I didn't cry, I discovered that, very, very slowly, I might actually be getting better.

It was Dad's ninety-fourth birthday on 12 March – the week after I finished my counselling sessions. In the past, Richard had always helped me organize a party for Dad. His neighbours and dancing friends would all turn up at his flat for glasses of wine and plates of smoked-salmon sandwiches. This year – with Richard not around to help – Dad asked me not to bother. Although I'd tried to shield him from the worst of my misery, he knew how unhappy I was, and, while he never said, I imagined he didn't want to put any extra burden on me.

But I decided this was the opportunity to try to prove to myself and to him that I was coping.

My brothers came to help with the party and, just as important, help restrain Dad from moving all the furniture around before the guests arrived. A crucial task after the occasion a few years ago, when Richard had turned his back for two minutes only to find Dad singlehandedly manhandling the sofa down the hallway just as the doorbell announced the first visitor. As my brothers and the girls whizzed around the room, pouring drinks and chatting, I saw Dad's face beaming over at me. Holding court from his favourite armchair and sipping a glass of red wine, he looked as content as I'd ever seen him.

When the guests had finally left, I brought him a cup of tea.

'It wasn't too bad without Richard, was it, Dad?'

'Oh, Richard,' he said in the tone of voice that meant: who's he? 'Do you know, I never give him a second thought.'

I believed him. Dad had chosen to behave as though Richard had never existed. I couldn't do the same – not when every inch of the house shrieked out memories at me, not when everything I did alone reminded me of everything we'd done together.

I embarked on an overhaul of the house. Every time I went to a gallery I bought a poster and framed it. Matisses, Picassos, Manets and Van Goghs soon adorned virtually every vertical surface – a small enough gesture, except that I had always bowed to Richard's spartan taste in the past. On a visit to Edinburgh, Bridget encouraged me to buy a set of girlie fairy lights to drape around the fireplace and a huge sparkling chandelier for the living room. I bought new bed linen and new china.

But the biggest and best thing I did was to get a dog. I'd always wanted a dog. So had the girls, but Richard had been dead set against it.

'It would be muggins here who'd have to walk it and clear up after it. I've got enough to do. The day a dog comes in, I walk out,' he would laugh. Only I knew he wasn't joking.

It might sound really trivial, but when I was ill, one of my big fears was that I would die without ever owning a dog. Now I could please myself, and I was bursting with excitement. So were the girls. We all knew that it heralded an entirely new chapter.

We spent weeks researching different breeds, unable to decide. Then one day I went to have lunch with Amanda. Bounding to meet me was her cockapoo – a cocker spaniel crossed with a poodle – Dylan, and I was bowled over. On the spur of the moment I borrowed Amanda's phone and rang Dylan's breeder, Lisa. When she said that she had six newborn puppies – all Dylan's half-brothers – it felt like fate. It seemed even more serendipitous when Lisa said we could pick our puppy up on 22 September – my fifty-first birthday. So that's the day that Elise and I drove to Wales and collected the puppy we had decided to call Milo.

It was a year to the day since that fateful birthday party when I'd tried to confront Richard about the affair, when he had lied and I had been so fragile and so powerless I had buried my head even deeper in the sand. And now here I was, cuddling a puppy, who looked like a curly little black lamb, and rejoicing that at last I could sense some happiness. And the strangest thing was that Milo made us feel like a family at last in a way we hadn't for a long, long time with Richard. Having Milo also made it easier when Ellen left for Rome where she had got a job as an au pair. A gap year postponed the awful moment when she would be leaving for her place at the Courtauld, but it was still a terrible wrench.

Milo had only been with us a week when I had to go out to do an interview. 'Bring him round here, I'll look after him,' said Dad eagerly, and he proceeded to spend a couple of exhausting hours chasing Milo around his flat.

When I finally arrived to relieve Dad, he was sound asleep in his armchair with Milo curled up at his feet.

'Ooh, that daft dog has led me a merry dance,' said Dad, pointing at Milo and the mounds of masticated newspaper littering the floor. If I could get into Milo's Bonio-sized brain, I'm sure I would discover that was the day my dog fell in love with my dad.

Dad is brusque, rough and ready, and not remotely sentimental around dogs, but he's always been fond of them. When they were little, my brothers had white mice called Persil and Omo after the washing powders. Dad used to clean the cages out with gritted teeth. After I was born, when they had more money, my parents bought a golden cocker spaniel which we called Sammy and treated like a mischievous baby brother. When Dad left for work in the morning, Mum would let Sammy bound on to Dad's chair and finish off the remains of his breakfast. When Dad came home at night, he would eye Sammy fiercely and go through a Three Bears style routine: 'I hope that bad dog hasn't been sitting in my chair.' And I would giggle so much I'd have to hide my face in Sammy's furry coat.

When Dad was posted to Germany, Sammy had to be rehomed. But as soon as we were settled back in England, my parents bought another cocker spaniel puppy, Patsy. She was supposed to be mine, but it was Dad who ended up uncomplainingly looking after her. He fed her, walked her and groomed her. The latter turned into a massive feat. With his huge hands, Dad's not the gentlest of men, and he's certainly not the most patient. Chasing Patsy around the garden when she needed grooming became a battle which Dad always lost. Once every couple of months, he would appear brandishing a huge pair of kitchen scissors and bellow: 'Come here, lass.' Patsy, who knew exactly what was in store, would instantly shoot under the nearest bush and it was left to me and whoever else was around to try and coax her out. When she was finally ensnared – usually by a huge pile of treats – Patsy would wriggle and squirm so much that Dad would finally have to admit defeat. She never, ever got her fur clipped properly.

Dad liked to claim that dogs should be like well-trained soldiers, jumping to attention at every order that was barked at them. But, in fact, he was far too soft-hearted to get angry with Patsy. Deep down, I think he's always enjoyed watching dogs have fun regardless of the mayhem they might be causing.

Now, Dad and Milo are pals. The relationship has been cemented by their joint fondness for Hobnobs. The day I finally banned Dad from sharing them with Milo was a sad one for both of them.

Milo helped transform our home after Richard left; and yet, however hard I tried to move on, one thing still haunted me.

And until I understood it, I knew I could never find total peace. Like a demented hamster racing around the same god-awful wheel, my poor exhausted brain trudged over the same old ground day in and day out. Why had I ignored what was going on for so long? Richard's betrayal was excruciatingly painful. But almost worse was knowing that I had effectively turned a blind eye. The clues were all there – and they were so obvious you wouldn't even dare offer them at a toddlers' treasure hunt. They were giant, neon billboards. And they'd all been flashing the same message: 'Open Your Eyes, Woman!'

I could understand – just about – how the affair had started, and I could forgive myself – just about – for being so trusting. Hindsight had done wonders in bringing every word, every nuance back to me. And I realized now that I had been standing at a crossroads the day Richard told me Karen had got upset and he had comforted her with a hug. In that physical gesture, a line was crossed and a professional relationship became a personal one.

In the split-second it took to weigh up the facts, my heart screamed out to trust him and that if I didn't, our marriage was worthless. He loved me and I loved him. I could have made a stand at any time, stopped him from working for Karen so much. But I didn't. I could have acted differently then. But I understood why I hadn't. However, I couldn't understand why, much later on, when my suspicions were aroused, I still refused to act. Why had I let him go waltzing off to the Caribbean?

Round and round the questions went. And I couldn't find an answer. And then one morning, when I was sharing a cup of tea with Dad, he reached out for a biscuit and a light went on in my head.

Every morning I fill the biscuit barrel on the little table beside his armchair with a selection of his favourite biscuits: bourbons, custard creams, jammy dodgers, chocolate digestives. By teatime they are usually all gone. When Dad first came to live with me, I assumed he had just been feeling particularly peckish after enduring relentlessly mediocre food at the care home. But the next day the same thing happened. I put in a whole packet of biscuits and by evening the barrel was empty.

'Dad, how many biscuits do you eat a day?' I asked.

'Oh, one or two,' Dad said, nonchalantly dipping a digestive into his cup of tea.

'But the biscuit barrel is empty,' I reasoned. 'And I put twelve in this morning – I counted.'

'Empty, you say?' he chuckled. 'Well, how about filling it up again, Tetty, love?'

Suddenly I understood. And the relief was indescribable. My love for Richard had made me too trusting for too long, that's for sure. But it was the cancer that made me bury my head in quick-dry cement. When I was ill, I didn't have a choice. It was a toss-up between confronting Richard with the truth or choosing to believe his lies. And I was pretty clear – even if I never, ever admitted it to myself – which one was more likely to help save my life. Without ever acknowledging it in so many words, I'd decided to believe his increasingly far-fetched tales, even though it meant lying to myself.

In doing so, I had done what my dad has been teaching me to do all my life. You deal with what you can and you leave the rest on the back-burner. When I'd been at my very lowest, I'd followed his example without even knowing it. And it had taken a biscuit barrel to get me to understand and forgive myself.

TWELVE

STEPPING INTO
THE UNKNOWN

As the months pass, Dad's self-protective skin is getting thicker. It has to. Dad's always been very clear-sighted about the passage of time. One of his favourite quotes in recent years has been from his beloved Shakespeare: the Seven Ages of Man speech from *As You Like It*:

> *Last scene of all,*
> *That ends this strange eventful history,*
> *Is second childishness and mere oblivion,*
> *Sans teeth, sans eyes, sans taste, sans everything.*

He quotes it with a certain amount of elan. And I know I'd find the truth of it much more distressing were Dad not so philosophical about the whole ageing process. He refuses to dwell on the fact that he will never again stroll into town, go dancing or even walk unaided across a room. He chooses not to think about all that he's lost. In fact, the most he will confess to me, on days when his knees are particularly

troublesome, is: 'Tessa, love, I'm beginning to feel my age.'
It's the same with all the other things Dad knows full well
but doesn't care to acknowledge. Even now he will regularly
wake from a nap in his armchair, look over at his walking
frame and wonder what on earth it's doing there. In his
head, he still sees himself as being able to leap up and run
down to the bottom of the garden.

'I've an idea that I'm not able to get around the way I
used to. Is that right or am I imagining it?' he asks.

'I'm afraid you are a bit wobbly on your feet these days,
Dad,' I remind him. When he totters to his feet and clings to
the frame, screwing up the courage to get going, it's like
watching an Olympic swimmer poised perilously on a diving
board ten metres up. And I can understand why he finds it
so much more pleasant to believe a different form of reality.
In certain circumstances, fibbing is a form of self-protection.

In truth, living with Dad is the nearest thing I can think
of to having a baby. Only instead of excitedly inching for-
wards, marking each new milestone, we are slowly but in-
exorably going backwards. The biggest change is that Dad is
beginning to have trouble using the toilet unaided. He can
make his way there with his walking frame, but he can't stand
up long enough to undo his trousers. Desperate for a solution, I bought Dad zipless jogging bottoms. He was horrified.

'These aren't proper trousers,' he sniffed. And I realized
that, however incapacitated he might be, he is still determined to cling on to certain standards.

So the jogging trousers went back to Marks and Spencer.

And, reluctantly, Dad has agreed that I can help him when he needs the loo. I've put an old-fashioned school bell in the bathroom so that he can ring when he needs me. Mum gave it to me so that I could call the girls in from the bottom of the garden. It gives a touch of *Downton Abbey* to the proceedings and makes me feel less like a carer. I'm Bates to Dad's Lord Grantham. I just need to work on the attentive manner.

'I'm sorry if I'm a bit of a pest, always wanting to go to the loo,' Dad apologizes quietly. 'I'm starting to think that I might be suffering from an old man's complaints.'

I say the only thing I can think of: 'Well, you are certainly a complaining old man, Dad.' He smiles, but we both know that there isn't really much humour in the situation.

If this all sounds tragic, it isn't meant to. Because, as with a baby, every stage is all-engrossing. Once it's passed, it's almost impossible to remember in any detail. Dad has been here ten months. I look back and I can't really remember. Was there a time when Dad read the newspaper? When he did the crossword? When he was eager to bound out of bed? When he didn't sleep most of the day? Maybe it's me protecting myself, too, because unless I try very hard, I can't clearly remember.

Dad claims to have no memory at all of being in hospital or of the six weeks he spent in a care home. I put it down to the fact that it was all such a shock and a period of his life he would rather forget. But it is odd. Even when we talk about it, no memories are prompted.

'Well, if you say I was there, love . . . ' and his voice tails off.

Often now he admits: 'I'm befuddled. My brain doesn't seem to be working.'

On Tuesday mornings, Helena comes as usual to give Dad Holy Communion.

'Who?' Dad asks when I mention her visit.

'You know, Dad. Helena. She comes every week.'

'Does she?' Dad looks puzzled.

'Yes, you like her very much. She was a teacher. We often say that she reminds you of Mum.'

Dad's face lights up with the happy memory. 'Of course. That's right.'

His religion is terribly important to him. During the war he carried a card stating that he was a Roman Catholic and asking that a priest be found to give him the last rites if he were mortally injured in battle. When I walk past the closed door, it's lovely to hear Helena and Dad repeating together the ancient prayers he once taught me. Helena's in her eighties, but she's bandbox smart, just like Mum always was. She's a wonderful raconteur with a most engaging way with words.

There are other puzzles too. One day in early summer, I'm talking about Mum's sister, Mary. She married a Canadian airman at the end of the war and went to live in Montreal – taking one of the first liners to cross the Atlantic after the war in 1946. My parents saw very little of her for many years. But Dad has always been extremely fond of her and, before he came to live with me, kept in touch regularly with phone calls and letters.

'I'm trying to think. I know the name, but who is Mary?' Dad asks hesitantly.

I'm stunned. He can't possibly have forgotten a woman he's known for over sixty years.

'Oh Dad, surely you know. Just have a little think.'

Dad shrugs crossly. 'Well, if you don't want to tell me . . .'

'It's not that I don't want to tell you, it's just that I think you ought to try and remember,' I respond in the snippy voice of the nasty, impatient teacher that seems to be lurking under the surface more and more often these days. But I can't stop myself.

We sit in a silence that seems interminable. Finally, Dad breaks it.

'Tetty, love, I didn't mean to upset you.' And I know then that he really doesn't remember, and I suspect that he's just as bewildered as I am by what's happening.

I kiss his cheek. 'I just want to help you, Dad.' But perhaps I don't always know the best way to help. To try and make amends, I reach up to the mantelshelf in Dad's room and take down the snapshot of my parents outside Mum's family home as they are about to set off for their honeymoon.

Dad's face lights up. He traces the figures with his finger. 'Oh yes, I remember – there's Mary in the front, pulling her big sister towards her honeymoon. Look on the back – Mum thought the pose was so funny she called it "The

Reluctant Bride".' Sure enough, there's the caption, just as Dad remembered. The memory's obviously there, just floating somewhere he can't always get to without help.

But the one person he unfailingly remembers and recognizes is Laura. In his mind, she's an old-school matron figure who unquestionably knows best, and he plays the role of recalcitrant schoolboy with gusto.

'You look like Mrs Tiggywinkle. Come on, James. Walk tall on your frame or you'll fall,' she admonishes as she follows him to the bathroom. Dad pulls a put-upon face but does as she suggests.

'Ooh, you're a bully,' he mutters.

'I know, I know. I torment you, don't I?' Laura says with her wonderfully infectious giggle that's more of a gurgle.

Laura may be fond of my dad, but she's got an equally soft spot for Milo. She's settling Dad into his chair for breakfast one morning when Milo pelts into the room.

'Come on, show us your tummy, Mile-o,' Laura urges, bending down to stroke him.

Dad pulls a mock scowl. 'You give all the attention to the bloody dog!'

'Yes, but he's got such a cute face.' Laura smiles back.

On another occasion, she's getting ready to leave when Milo hurls himself at her. As she crouches on the floor to tickle him, Dad looks bemused. 'Soft lass, spoiling that daft dog,' he mutters to himself.

Laura shoots him a look as if to say: 'You've got a point

there.' Then she's on her feet and rushing over to tickle Dad. 'We can't have you getting jealous, James!' she laughs.

As he gets frailer, Dad is increasingly disinclined to do things for himself. Every morning, once he's out of bed, he looks beseechingly at Laura, hoping she will help him on with his slippers.

'Come on, good girl,' he wheedles.

Laura is firm. 'Now, James, you are perfectly capable of putting them on yourself,' she says crisply.

Dad grimaces, but he knows when he's beaten.

When Laura takes a week's holiday, we both miss her terribly and Dad is delighted to get a postcard from Blackpool. 'I hope you are being a good boy for the other pyjama girls,' she has written. He is even more chuffed when she returns with a huge box of fudge for him.

In Laura's absence, we get a stand-in carer for the mornings and the few evenings she does. The first morning as he gets out of bed, I notice that his pyjama trousers are on back to front.

'Someone must have been playing a practical joke on me,' he mutters. 'I got up in the night to try and use the loo and I found I was all buttoned up wrong.' He's not even remotely irritated. Just amused.

I check the notes that the carer – a pretty Chinese girl called Gwen – had made in Dad's folder the previous night.

'Helped James into his nightie,' she has written. When I tell Dad, he roars with laughter. We decide that this must be the first time she had got an elderly gentleman ready for bed and didn't fully understand the intricacies of male attire.

As with a baby, I'm spending more of every day caring about Dad, thinking about Dad, worrying about Dad. When Dad first moved in, I would cheerfully leave him alone for half a day with a Thermos flask of tea and a plate of sandwiches. I knew he would be safe and happy. Now I'm much less confident.

The truth is that this is completely uncharted territory for both of us. I never had grandparents living with me – I never even met Dad's parents, and I only dimly remember Mum's because they both died when I was five, within six weeks of each other. My only prior experience of caring is of being a mum and that came with an instruction manual. In fact, a whole IKEA Billy bookcase full of them. When you have a baby, you're swamped with advice from every conceivable quarter. Even the most cursory acquaintance suddenly feels they've got the right to browbeat you with tips. Not to mention all those parenting magazines and baby manuals offering advice so contradictory that it's enough to make you feel like Alice in Wonderland, shipped up uninvited at the Mad Hatter's tea party and presented with one mind-boggling riddle after another. Feeding on demand. Controlled crying. Naughty steps and potty training. There's a view on everything and a definitive answer to nothing.

But when an elderly parent comes to live with you, you're very much on your own. There are no manuals with titles such as *How to Have a Happy, Healthy Granddad*, or

Contented Old Codger. It's a relief in one way, alarming in another. It has meant that Dad and I are left to stumble along in the dark. It's companionable, but it's certainly not glitch-free.

When Dad first moved in, I was determined to keep him on his toes. For his sake? For mine? I'm not quite sure. I badgered him to do things he used to enjoy, such as reading the paper and doing the crossword. Dad went along with it all gamely, but, deep down, he knew it was a losing battle. Actually, that's too negative a description for what was going on in his head. I think Dad had decided he had seen quite enough warfare, thank you very much, and this was a battle best avoided.

'How are you getting on with your book, Dad?' I'd ask, clocking that the bookmark sticking out of his large-print library copy of Vera Lynn's autobiography *We'll Meet Again* hadn't moved in days.

'It's interesting enough,' Dad replied.

'But you don't seem to be reading very much,' I persisted. 'Would you like me to get you something different? More historical? More of a story?'

'I wouldn't bother. I'm enjoying it well enough,' Dad said, making a show of reaching out for the book, just to please me. Or was it to placate me?

And, ten minutes later, there the book would be – on Dad's chest while he snoozed gently and I fumed quietly.

What was happening to my once tack-sharp dad?

It was the same with television programmes. Dad used to watch the news avidly, only halting for his daily dose of *Deal or No Deal* or a Second World War documentary on the History Channel. Now the television is rarely on. Dad simply doesn't have the interest to watch or the energy to concentrate. Like a hectoring head girl, I tried to gee Dad up to do things I thought were good for him. But like the bad boy at the back of the class, he was happier throwing paper darts.

I'd put the TV guide by Dad's armchair, open at the day's page. When that didn't work, I ringed programmes I thought he might enjoy (OK, I own up – programmes that sounded stimulating). When Dad still refused to display any interest, I took to switching the television on for the news. He responded by instantly falling into a deep sleep.

'But Dad, you used to be so interested in current affairs. What's happened?' I complained.

Dad shrugged. 'I'm happy in my own little way.' And I knew then what he really meant was: 'Leave me alone.'

And then I remember that, when I was ill, I couldn't be bothered with an awful lot of things, either. I only had limited resources and I wasn't going to waste them on anything that didn't make me feel healthier or happier. From the day I was diagnosed, I didn't read a single newspaper. I opted for trash and trivia on TV and made a deliberate decision not to tax my brain by trying to remember anything that wasn't absolutely necessary. So what if Dad's taking the same attitude? It's not as though he's ever going to want to run a marathon or win *Mastermind*. The truth is that, without any fuss or fanfare, he's quietly but very consciously preparing for death. When he's not sleeping, he's spending most of the time thinking back over his life or saying his prayers. Books and TV are a distraction from the important things going on in his head.

I'm not quite sure what I should be doing. I'm not even quite sure how to describe what it is that I'm doing. The vocabulary is woefully inadequate. There's a verb for being a mother. But there's no such word as daughtering. 'I daughter, you daughter, she daughters' doesn't really trip off the tongue. However, the reality is that that's exactly what I'm doing. I'm daughtering my dad. What else could I call it? I'm a mother to the girls, but I'm definitely not mothering Dad. Neither of us would want that. I care about him. But am I actually being a carer for him? Is that my role now? I'm not sure. We don't have the vocabulary. We don't have the guide book. We don't have the know-how. And yet women my age are finding ourselves thrust into this new daughtering role. Sons too.

When I talk it over with my brothers, they're as much in the dark as I am. We all agree that it would be good for Dad to stay mobile and mentally agile – but how far do we push him? Does he still know what's best for himself? Do we? As Dad is becoming frailer and needing more help – particularly when using the bathroom – Andy has been visiting more regularly. He's an artist, so he can work just as well in my home as in his, and as he's single, he's free to come and go as he pleases. Sometimes he comes for a long weekend, which is lovely. I'm happy to leave Dad alone for a few hours during the day while I go shopping or meet friends for coffee, but I'm reluctant to leave him alone in the evening until he's settled in bed, in case he falls on his way there. So, if I have a dinner party or a trip to the cinema arranged, Andy's prepared to hold the fort.

We have very different styles with Dad. I'm brusque. Andy is indulgent. I'm sure it's partly down to my style of mothering. But it's also down to our relationship with Dad. Maybe because I'm the youngest and a girl, I've never felt in awe of Dad. My brothers are much more wary of upsetting him than I am. Dad is eager to spoil me and still wants to protect me, just because I'm a girl.

Andy happens to be staying when, one morning in early July, Dad is walking along the hallway from his bedroom to the bathroom and his knees buckle. He falls on to the tiled floor. Luckily, nothing is broken, but Dad's skin is now as thin as tracing paper. And the slight cut on his elbow looks as though he's been hacked at with a machete. Dad is shaking with shock. Between us, Andy and I manage to lift Dad into his wheelchair. He is patched up in A & E, but the incident triggers off memories of his fall the previous summer. It leaves him very shaken and convinced he's done some terrible damage to himself. Overnight he seems to age another ten years as all his confidence ebbs away.

'I've fractured my elbow,' he tells Laura weakly the next morning. 'I'm a nuisance. I should be in a home.'

I've never heard him talk like this before, and it's worrying. Laura cheerfully teases him: 'Don't worry, James. If you were a nuisance, Tessa would soon cart you off.'

Dad's never been given to over-dramatizing ill health, so the suggestion that he might want to be in a care home is a sign of just how frightening he found the incident and how scared he is that it might happen again. I'm not sure whether he feels he's putting an unnecessary burden on me or whether he feels insecure. Whichever it is, it's not ideal. And I find that we might be entering a new chapter in which Dad will need me even more.

I was at a dinner party recently and found myself sitting between two men in their early fifties. Ruefully, I explained my family set-up – Dad, daughters, dog. They were riveted. Not, sadly, because I'm a single, solvent woman with sex appeal, but because they hoped I might throw some light on their own troubles.

Michael's father has recently been diagnosed with Alzheimer's. Michael is desperate to move him nearer, but his dad – who doesn't accept that there's anything wrong with him – is reluctant to leave the family home, even though it's falling down around his ears. So Michael makes a hundred-mile round trip once a week to visit him and is frantically trying to organize carers who are prepared to put up with a cantankerous, confused old man swearing at them and accusing them of stealing the ashtrays (particularly odd as he's never smoked in his life). Poor Michael knows it's only a stop-gap, but the prospect of trying to coax his father into a care home fills him with dread.

Colin's mum has been in a care home ever since she had a stroke three months ago. He hates visiting her because every time he tries to leave she begs him to take her home. The staff are kind, but the other elderly residents are so mentally confused they frighten her.

'So how do you make it work?' they asked in unison.

What could I say? There are so many answers. I've got the room. I've got the time. I've got wonderful family support. I've got fantastic carers. I've got a sweet-natured, easy-going dad. I love the way Dad makes me feel useful and appreciated. I don't have a demanding husband. I don't have children who need my full attention. I don't have to go out to an office every day. And Dad himself is such a joy. He's physically frail but as much himself as he ever was. Are these all the essential components or just some of them? Honestly, I don't know.

Living with Dad is working so well that I take care not to sound smug. Soon after Dad arrived, Mum's friend Betty, who's lived alone since her husband died some ten years ago, began to need help from carers. She's been part of my life forever and I ring occasionally to pass on family news.

One morning, a carer picks up the phone. She is brusque and sounds harassed. When I ask if she can help Betty to get to the phone, it's obvious that she thinks it's a terrible imposition. And when Betty does finally pick up, she can't work out who I am because she hasn't got her hearing aids in. I hear her calling out anxiously: 'What do I do? Can you help me?'

The carer's voice booms in the background. 'I'm sorry, Elizabeth. There's no time. I've got to go. They'll have to ring back later when you've found your hearing aids.'

And that's it. With a squeak of apology, Betty hangs up, leaving me feeling sad and helpless. I think of how vulnerable she must feel. I think of our lovely carers, who always behave as if they have all the time in the world. Dad tuts. 'She ought to be living with her family.'

I know it's not as simple as that. Betty's daughter, Clare, lives nearby. But I've got the impression over the years that Betty and her son-in-law don't get on. Back in the day, Betty didn't make any secret of the fact that she disapproved of him. The bitterness has been papered over, but it's never disappeared.

I'm relieved when, a few weeks later, Clare rings to say that her mum is moving into a care home. At £800 a week, the fees are eye-wateringly steep. Clare notices my sharp intake of breath.

'I know, it's outrageous, isn't it? And what makes it even worse is that Mum doesn't even want to go there. In fact, she's kicking up a hell of a fuss. She wants her independence. But what can we do? She can't manage by herself any more. She's barely eating because she can't be bothered to cook. And she can't come and live with us. She knows that. We'd drive each other mad.

'Um,' I agree.

'So how's it going with you and Jimmy? All still OK? No regrets?'

Oh, Lord. This is tough. 'Fine so far,' I say, trying to temper my enthusiasm. 'But Dad is still able to be active, which makes things much easier. And he's so appreciative . . . ' The rest of the sentence hangs in the air.

'So he should be. He's very lucky. But don't let him take over your life,' says Clare as she rings off.

It's a bitter little warning, but I'm not surprised. I heard it a lot before Dad moved in when I was explaining my plans. 'Wow –' long pause '– You're terribly brave', and I knew what people really wanted to say was: 'My God, have you completely lost your marbles?' It wasn't exactly comforting.

One of Dad's neighbours even took me to one side to warn me: 'My sister-in-law took my father in and it almost killed her. That old man was so demanding. By the end she was having to bathe him and toilet him and there wasn't a shred of gratitude. I know your dad's a sweet old man, but people can get very selfish, you know. I'm sure you know what you are doing. But don't feel you have to sacrifice your own life, my dear. You really don't.'

I was taken aback. I didn't see Dad coming to live with me as a sacrifice. It seemed to be the ideal arrangement for both of us. But was I missing something crucial? Was I being wildly, wilfully obtuse?

I guess because my mother had died so quickly, slipping away without any trauma, and because Dad was in such rude health, it had never occurred to me to fear Dad's future or my part in it. In fact, I was blissfully oblivious to the whole issue of ageing parents until I started telling people about my new living arrangements. Then it struck me that, whether we love our parents passionately or merely tolerate them, when we reach our fifties, or even before we do, most of us live in a state of uneasy anxiety about them. When are they going to die? What's going to happen before they die? And what on earth are we going to be called upon to do about it all?

Sometimes I wonder how I would have managed if I'd had to look after Mum instead of Dad. I adored her, but could we have shared a house just as comfortably? Would she have let me look after her so readily? Would I have been able to 'daughter' her when she had always been so much of a mother to me? The truth is that I still find it almost impossible to imagine my mum as anything but formidable and indefatigable. Although she lived with the knowledge that she was dying for four months, she didn't allow me or any of us to glimpse even the slightest trace of frailty or fear until right at the end.

The first time I saw how weak she was, we were Christmas shopping together for the girls. It was three weeks before Christmas and the toy shop was unbearably hot and crowded. Mum – who always hated crowds – was behind me as I tried to manoeuvre a path through. I turned and instinctively I took her hand to protect her. It was exactly the same gesture I used to keep Ellen or Elise close to me and I felt a surge of a new and totally different sort of love for Mum. And that's what I still felt when, on Christmas Day, Mum felt so ill she left us opening the presents without her while she went back to bed. When I went up to check on her, she looked so frightened that I did something I'd never done before: I made a decision for her. I rang the hospital and asked them to take her in. She was too frail to even notice that I had taken charge. Safe and well cared for, she died nine days later. But now I wonder whether she would have coped as well as Dad has with a gradual leeching-away of her independence. Or how well I would have coped.

I barely have one female friend who isn't struggling to know what to do for the best for an ageing parent. It seems only yesterday we were comparing notes about potty training and play groups, Kumon Maths classes and clarinet tutors. Now we talk with unashamedly grisly interest about bowel movements (not our own, I hasten to add; that would be really peculiar) and care homes, about the best ways to release equity in the family home and how to access Meals on Wheels. There are some fundamental differences, of course. We swop stories, we sigh and we laugh about our parents' peculiarities, but the one thing we never, ever do is try and compete. Who would want to? We are only too aware that it isn't an upward trajectory and there are no prizes for being precocious. We're not boasting about miraculous Jemima, not quite two yet, asking for an avocado – by name. We're not reporting how Sam knows his entire times table from beginning to end although he's barely five. In fact, we are doing the exact opposite. We are listening in horror and waiting in dread for things to get worse.

'Mum rang me in the middle of the night. She thought it was the afternoon. She couldn't remember where she'd left her false teeth and was worried the dog had eaten them.' It doesn't quite have the same impressive ring as: 'Jasper has just won first prize in the county chess championship.'

So I know, without a shadow of a doubt, how lucky I am that Dad came to live with me at just the right time for both of us – when I needed him most, when I could be most useful to him.

THIRTEEN

WORK? WHAT'S THAT?

It's 9 p.m. Rebecca, Dad's carer, has just left and I've popped in to kiss Dad goodnight. I check that his toes are nice and warm and that he has a hankie under his pillow. As I reach the door, I turn. Dad beams at me and waves his hand like a little child. 'Night, night,' he mouths.

'Sleep tight,' I reply. And then I remember: 'I won't be here in the morning, Dad,' I explain. 'I'm off to London for the day. Andy will give you breakfast.'

Dad's smile broadens. 'You have fun. Don't worry about me.'

And I won't, because, seamlessly, things have moved on to a different stage. Andy has moved in to help.

When Dad first came to live with me, I airily imagined that I would carry on working from home pretty much as normal. Having Dad parked comfortably in his armchair couldn't be any harder than having a toddler rampaging around, I reasoned. When Ellen was born, I was working as a feature writer on the *Sun*. I'd joined in 1986. Freddie Starr had just eaten someone's hamster and the *Sun* was Britain's bestselling daily newspaper. Working within screaming distance of larger-than-life characters such as show-business editor Piers Morgan was exhilarating, terrifying and exhausting in equal measures. And when Ellen arrived, I knew without a shadow of a doubt that I didn't want that life any more.

I couldn't see myself ever again being willing to shoot off at a moment's notice to prowl the late-night streets of Benidorm looking for drunken Brits (how tame that all seems now). I didn't fancy any more evenings standing in foul-smelling public phone boxes in the middle of dodgy London council estates dictating pages of notes with the sound of the news editor bellowing in the background that the presses were about to roll. I couldn't picture myself hanging around nightclubs at 2 a.m. hoping to get an interview with Boy George, Toyah Willcox, or any of the other flamboyantly famous stars of the eighties. And, after flying into Prague in December 1989 with a Page Three girl and a suitcase crammed with newspapers specially printed in Czech welcoming the country to democracy, I reckoned I'd done my bit for international relations. But, most of all, I couldn't bear to leave Ellen for an hour, let alone a whole day.

So, in 1991, I left the *Sun* to work as a freelance feature writer for magazines and newspapers. For the last twelve years I've written almost exclusively for the *Daily Mail*. Working from home sounds idyllic, and it is in very many ways. I've never had to commute into an office. I've never had to abandon the girls for days at a time to disappear on a foreign trip. But throw in newspaper deadlines, last-minute jobs and interviews overrunning, and life was one long race just to stay upright. The girls were all too often the last children in the playground, waiting forlornly to be picked up because I was stuck on the end of a phone. They would say that there wasn't a single parents' evening where they didn't face the embarrassment of me having to dash off to answer an urgent call from an editor. And I probably missed more Christmas parties, sports days and music concerts than I ever attended. Mercifully, they don't seem to remember all the occasions when I plonked them in a playpen or shoved them into a pram and pushed them to the bottom of the garden where no one could hear them scream, then fled back to my desk to do a phone interview.

I love my career and I'm proud of my work and the lifestyle it's given the girls. And by the time Dad moved in, all those fraught moments were a distant memory. For almost a year, I managed to carry on as normal. But over the last few months, Dad has started getting more dependent and the person he wants to depend on isn't me. It's Andy. Dad doesn't really like to have me help him on and off the loo. Carers are for that. Or chaps. And in front of them, Dad feels blissfully free to vent his frustration when his body won't do what he wants.

I don't want to imply that Dad is given to swearing. Far

from it. The thought of the F-word ever passing his lips is inconceivable. But there is one notable exception. He has always had a penchant for the word 'bugger', as in 'You silly bugger', or even, on occasion 'Oh bugger me!' Unfortunately, he introduced the word to Mum, who used it with enthusiastic abandon all through my childhood until the fateful day when Dad felt he had to own up to what it really meant. My convent-educated mum, who even drew the line at saying 'damn' out of religious propriety, almost collapsed on the spot. She couldn't have been more shocked if she'd just discovered that she'd spent the last twenty years without any knickers on.

Dad has been anxious about falling again ever since his tumble earlier in the summer. When the doctor called to check up on his recovery, he was reassuring.

'There's no reason why it should happen again, Mr Cunningham. The best thing you can do is to keep moving, even if it's only doing little exercises in your chair to keep the circulation going.'

Dad looked unconvinced. So was I. The truth is that Dad spends so much of the time snoozing that, when he wakes up, he's unsure whether minutes have passed or whole hours, and it takes him a while to sort out fact from dream in his head. Nevertheless, determined to help keep him mobile, I took the doctor's advice and bought a wind-up egg timer which would ping to alert Dad whenever it was time to hop out of his chair and march up and down on the spot – supposedly excellent exercise for elderly chaps who are largely chair-bound. I put the timer prominently beside Dad's armchair and set it to go off in thirty minutes. He seemed unenthusiastic but promised he would give it a go. Reassured, I disappeared off to my study, next to Dad's room, convinced that I had a clear space for some uninterrupted work. Thirty minutes later, I was on the phone, interviewing an eminent scientist about the complexities of fish oils, when through the wall came the sound of the pinging alarm clock. I was pleased.

Now Dad will do some exercise, I thought.

But, to my horror, the ping was followed by a blast of 'Bugger me!' Then, as I threw myself and the phone under the desk to try and muffle the sound, there was an outraged yell: 'Tessa? Tessa! What the hell's going on?'

'Um, I think someone might be calling you,' my po-faced scientist said crisply as I tried to think of some polite way of winding up the interview.

This was intolerable. I marched next door, determined to tear a strip off Dad for shouting the house down. But I'd barely opened my mouth when my anger evaporated. He'd just woken up and was so obviously befuddled and confused by the strange noise that all I could do was hug him and suggest a cup of tea.

A few days later, I set up a phone interview for 4 p.m. At 3.54 precisely, Dad suddenly announced that he needed to go to the bathroom. We had six minutes. It should be enough time. And it was. Just. Dad was back in his armchair at 4 p.m. precisely.

'Everything fine, Dad?'

'Yes, lovely.'

'OK. Then I'm just going next door to do my phone interview.'

'Clever girl. Just one thing, Tetty?'

'Yes?'

'I need to go to the loo again . . . '

I realized then that we were entering a whole new phase. And I was woefully unprepared. How was I going to work? How was I going to earn money? When Dad came to live with me, I was aware that it was a step into the unknown. Even so, I hadn't accounted for Dad becoming quite so needy quite so quickly. And I didn't want to be sucked back into my old life. When the girls were little, I'd been so busy juggling that I'd never stepped back to see just what a muddle it all was. It took me falling ill to take a long, hard look at what my life was like. And I vowed that I would never put myself under that level of stress again. But here I was and it seemed that I didn't have a choice. Or did I?

It's a cliché that no one's last words are ever: 'I wish I'd spent more time in the office.' But when you're caught up in your career, it's almost impossible to imagine a time will ever come when work doesn't matter a damn. But that time is definitely here for Dad. And, actually, it always has been.

Dad is utterly convinced that everyone needs to be gainfully employed and to feel useful. If he'd had the chance, he'd have rushed back to work just to fill the hole after Mum died. But, at eighty, even he had to admit that it might be a bit much for him. Dad was obviously a much-loved teacher. There are still ex-pupils – some of them now grand-parents – who greet him fondly in the street. Dad, like so many other autodidacts, has always been passionate about education. However, his ambition was never to be the best teacher on the planet. He simply wanted to provide the best he could for his family. Of all the episodes in his life that he enjoys talking about, he never talks about his job. His job never defined him and it certainly doesn't now.

Dad always put his family before everything, and certainly before his career. Simon was about to sit the eleven-plus when Dad's boss in the Army Education Corps asked him to move to another base. It would mean new schools for us all. Dad refused.

'We're both teachers. Surely you understand how important my son's education is right now?' he argued.

His commanding officer didn't. In fact, he was so annoyed that he wrote a damning annual report on Dad. 'Not fit for promotion.'

'The real army man jumps to attention and does exactly what he's told – and that wasn't me,' Dad said, shrugging. He never got to rise above the rank of captain.

On top of my work, I was juggling the jobs of mother one minute and daughter the next. I became reluctant to leave Dad for more than a few hours, but, one day in August, I had no choice. Elise was taking a final look at universities. She had an offer from Birmingham, but she wasn't sure about it. The deadline for her decision was looming and the only way to decide was to take a day trip. That meant that while I was in Birmingham, Ellen, who was home for the holidays, was going to have to look after Dad. She would be twenty in two days. She's been an au pair. She's perfectly capable. Even so, as we got ready to catch the early-morning train, I had an uneasy feeling that this wasn't what I ought to be doing: Dad was my responsibility.

I couldn't shake off the feeling of unease. It didn't help us enjoy Birmingham. Sure enough, I got home that night to find Ellen upset and Dad anxious and disorientated.

When he saw me, his face lit up with a smile of relief. Ellen was less easy to comfort.

'Grandpa swore at me. He called me a "silly bugger". I didn't know what to do,' she says, between sobs. I know, from the way she says it, that she finds it almost impossible to believe and a sick feeling of guilt wells up in me. 'I told him that supper was ready, but he wanted to go into the garden. So I was trying to put his hat on but I got it back to front. He got really cross. And then, when Grandpa went to the loo and I left him, he started shouting out: "Pyjama Girl! Carer! Anyone!"' She shudders.

'Don't blame Grandpa. He was frightened.'

'Oh, I don't blame him. I know it's not his fault – but it was horrible. He didn't want me to help him and I didn't know what to do.'

I could see it all. Dad feeling helpless. Dad not wanting to rely on his granddaughter. Dad wanting to protect her from his needs. Dad shielding himself by pretending to himself that she was a professional carer, not the little girl he used to cuddle on his lap.

I felt angry with myself. I hadn't just short-changed them. I'd robbed them: Ellen of her innocence, Dad of his security.

It was a turning point. I decided that I was going to have to think of a better way.

I was happy for Dad to be my priority for as long as he needed to be. Even so, the prospect of letting go of my career altogether, or placing too much responsibility on the girls to make up the shortfall in my time, was scary. And then two things happened. An agent saw an article I had written in the *Daily Mail* about Dad coming to live with me and suggested that my experiences might provide the basis for a book. I was intrigued but couldn't imagine how I'd ever find the time.

While I was thinking it over, I went on holiday to New York with the girls to stay with their cousins, Simon's sons, Carlos and George. Andy offered to move in to look after Dad while we were away. I was grateful. But, along with the relief and the excitement of tasting total freedom again, I must admit that I was slightly apprehensive. I was so used to looking after Dad by myself that leaving him felt like leaving Ellen at nursery for the first time. I rang every day. Although Dad is too deaf to manage phone calls, it was good to hear Andy's reassuring voice.

When I came home, Dad was blissfully content, his skin glowing from afternoons spent snoozing in the garden. Andy was bursting with stories of the fun they'd had. Even Milo looked chipper. And, as for me – I'd decided I'd like to write the book. Andy was due to leave as soon as he'd handed his duties over to me. But one day drifted into the next. When Andy finally left in early October, after three weeks of Dad-sitting, the house seemed suddenly quiet. Dad seemed a little lost. Instinctively, when he needed help in the bathroom, it was Andy's name he called, not mine.

'I've come to depend on Andy,' he admitted.

When Andy rang to check up on Dad a few days later, I told him how much he was missed. 'Dad really loved having you here. The more often you can visit, the happier he'll be. We all will.' I wasn't planning to guilt-trip him. After all, it had been my decision to have Dad live with me.

There was a long silence. 'Well,' Andy finally said. 'I'm pleased to hear that, because I really enjoyed spending time with Dad. It was a total pleasure. I've been wondering whether it might be helpful if I came and stayed more often and for longer?'

I tried to keep the eagerness out of my voice. 'You mean, sort of living between here and Brighton?'

'Well, yes. Perhaps even living more at your place, if that's OK.'

'But that's wonderful. Yes please. Definitely. We don't need to set anything in stone. We can try it and see what happens.'

*

Andy moved into the spare bedroom in October. Leaving his home and putting his old life on hold is a big sacrifice, but it's one he's prepared to make for Dad and me. So far, apart from occasional trips back to Brighton, he has been here ever since. All of a sudden, living with Dad now involves living with my brother as well. Odd when you think we haven't shared a house since he was twenty-one and I was thirteen. Even then it was only part time, because he was at university. Even odder that it seems to work.

I bite my lip about his smoking. He pretends not to notice my bossiness. I tease him when he insists on popping ice cubes and a slice of lemon into the glass of water he brings Dad every lunchtime, the glass Dad stalwartly refuses to drink. Andy shares all the mundane jobs, from taking the bins out to cleaning Dad's hearing aids, a weekly task involving a lot of soapy water, a paper clip (trust me, you don't want to know more) and endless patience. He treats Dad to two puddings with custard every single day – one for lunch, one for supper. 'You're going to spoil him,' I warn. Then I realize how ridiculous that sounds.

I find it immensely moving to watch the tender way in which Andy treats Dad. From somewhere – God knows where – Andy seems to have acquired a caring gene which has passed the rest of the family by. Throughout my entire life he's spoilt me. But to watch Dad allowing himself to be pampered by Andy for the first time in both their lives is incredibly sweet.

Every night, Andy drapes Dad's pyjamas over the radiator

to warm them, and after breakfast, he settles him in his armchair with a fresh cup of tea. If I'm not there to raise a mocking eyebrow, Andy even operates the controls of Dad's special reclining armchair for him. Dad, who has always been so gruff with the boys, so indulgent of everyone but himself, laps it all up.

Unexpected as it is, it works, because although Andy is eight years older than me, and until now we've led totally separate and very different lives, we have always been close. It was Andy who took me to the cinema for the first time (to see *The Jungle Book*) and bought us both chips to eat in the street afterwards – swearing me to silence and to promise not to tell Mum. It was Andy who bought me my first grown-up dress to go to my first disco, and it was Andy who, when I was sick, sent me lovely funny cards, books and DVDs to cheer me up.

Andy and I share tasks – sometimes disastrously. One day Andy was helping me make supper. He was about to mash the potatoes when Dad called. Andy bounded upstairs to the ground floor, so I took over, emptying half a carton of cream into the potatoes. I was checking on the meat in the oven when Andy raced back into the kitchen. My back was turned as he grabbed the saucepan of mashed potato, poured half a pint of milk into it, followed by an egg and a slab of butter, then dashed back upstairs again.

'Lovely mashed potato,' said Dad. 'Who made it?'

'I did,' we answered together. It may have been a heart attack on a plate, but Dad eagerly lapped up every bit.

Dad's love affair with food is a revelation. His three meals are the highlights of his day – punctuated by the droplets of pleasure provided by frequent cups of tea, biscuits and Mr Kipling cakes.

'Ooh, lovely, darling,' he'll chirrup like a little bird receiving a titbit.

I always thought Dad was indifferent to food – that's certainly the impression he gave when I was growing up. He would eat Mum's frugal speciality for Good Friday – tinned pilchards, mashed potato and peas – with the same relish he reserved for cakes and crumbles.

As children, Mum allowed us one pet hate each. I was allowed not to eat tomatoes. Simon chose pineapple. Andy, unaccountably, chose chocolate cake. Absolutely everything else, from rock-hard liver to soggy cabbage, we had to eat. Dad, meanwhile, gamely claimed there was not a single dish of Mum's that he didn't enjoy. He didn't want anyone ever accusing him of being like his father, who turned mealtimes into purgatory with his complaints about Grandma's cooking. But Dad was never lavish in his praise. Perish the thought. Mum believed that showing too much interest in food was vulgar. In fact, in our family, there were three subjects that were off limits: sex, money and food. As a child, I assumed this was a rule that Mum had got from the Pope – the one person on earth she seemed in awe of. Having met lots of priests since, I think it was just one of her quirks.

Everything apart from food – politics, religion, personal

relationships – was open to exhaustive discussion at the dinner table. 'Putting the world to rights,' Dad called it as he ambled off to get on with the washing-up while Mum got stuck into the long debates she loved. I'm grateful to my parents for not talking about money. It left us all feeling we were very comfortably off, whereas, in reality, we definitely weren't – or at least not until my parents were well into their fifties and Mum was working. But I wish I'd known more about sex and food. Finding out about the first wasn't a hardship, but I rather resent all the time I wasted not knowing that discussing food and being knowledgeable about it adds hugely to the enjoyment of it. All those years, Dad was obviously burning to voice his appreciation of food. Because where once he ate every single thing uncomplainingly, now he leaves me in absolutely no doubt about his tastes.

He's suspicious of all vegetables except peas and cauliflower cheese, and the longer he's been living with me, the more marked his dislike has become. He particularly dislikes broad beans, cabbage and salad of any kind. He loves shepherd's pie, cottage pie – indeed anything mushy. And he loves all puddings, everything from spotted dick to blackberry crumble. And always with a huge dollop of either ice-cream or custard. Anything less and he feels cheated.

However, years of practice mean Dad can't actually bring himself to admit that he doesn't like vegetables or – and I feel I'm telling tales here – can't be bothered to eat them. So he came up with an excuse: his dentures. I'm sure it started innocently enough. Dad genuinely began to find it increasingly hard to chew meat. Roast dinners were out of the question. But soon even casseroles presented a problem. Dad would push the meat around his plate with a disconsolate-looking face. I was disappointed for him, slightly irritated for myself, and worried about what on earth we were going to do about this. While at the beginning it was OK to grind up the occasional meal for Dad's comfort, it seemed to be getting out of hand. There's a lot Elise has been prepared for since Dad moved in, but she'd draw the line at being force-fed cottage pie seven days a week.

I still maintain that we should eat together at least a few times a week. That's what families do. But, reluctantly, I have started stocking up on supermarket ready meals for Dad to eat by himself – all the kinds of sloppy food he eats with alacrity. For family meals, I resurrect old favourites not seen so often since I was a hard-up student with no money and no clue how to cook: spag bol, chilli con carne, toad in the hole and (heaven help us) faggots. It's more fun than I'd expected and a damn sight cheaper.

Even so, as Dad hands me his plate at the end of a meal, completely clean except for the untouched vegetables, he offers a shrug of apologetic disappointment. For extra measure, he sighs: 'I'd love to eat them, darling, particularly when you've gone to so much trouble, but they're too hard for me. I just can't manage them.'

Since Andy has been here, the number of vegetables that Dad can't eat has been growing so alarmingly that we got quite concerned. So in November we booked an appointment with the dentist. If Dad can't even eat a soft-boiled carrot, something must be very wrong with his dentures. The dentist offered a full examination. Dad wasn't keen. 'No need to bother. I've only had these dentures five minutes.' Actually, he's had them for two years.

But I understood the reason for his reluctance when the dentist beckoned Andy and me into the consulting room.

'I've told Mr Cunningham that his dentures are a perfect fit and in extremely good condition. He obviously looks after them very well.' He beamed while Dad looked shame-faced in the corner. He knew he'd been rumbled.

After that I refused to listen to any more lame excuses. But the final straw came a few weeks later. We always eat Sunday lunch together – Andy, Dad, Elise and me – gathered around the table in Dad's room. This Sunday I cooked roast pork. Without thinking, I served Dad some crackling. Without thinking, he popped it in his mouth and was soon chewing away contentedly.

Elise's eyes met mine in stunned astonishment. Then she started giggling. So did Andy and I.

'Grandpa, you old fraud,' Elise snickered.

Dad knew that he'd been caught out. And he took up his default position when in trouble with a female: flattery – lavish, totally over the top and completely irresistible.

'But the crackling looked so delicious, I just couldn't resist,' he said, smiling.

As one of us is at home virtually all the time now, Dad doesn't need the lunchtime call. So we cancel it and bump

Dad's morning visit from Laura up from thirty to forty-five minutes instead. As it becomes harder and harder to winkle my dad out of bed, we increase it again to a full hour to give Laura plenty of time. The last thing I want is for her to feel pressured or under stress. They have such a lark together.

One morning, I watch her gently tap him awake. He beams up at her. The curtains are open. Sun is shining into the room, but Dad's reluctant to move.

'I'm so comfortable here.'

'I can see you are, James,' she says, patting the duvet down and tucking him in.

Dad blinks apprehensively at her. He suspects what's coming. Sure enough, with one sudden movement, Laura whips the duvet off.

'Oh, you cruel woman.'

'Nicey, nicey just doesn't work with you,' she laughs, wagging her finger.

But although Dad is depending more and more on us physically, there are still some things on which he won't be overruled. And that is how it should be.

The autumn has been glorious and Dad has been able to sit outside many more days than I dared hope. But finally, in late October, Andy and I pack the garden furniture away. The barbecue goes under wraps. The parasol disappears into the shed.

Then one morning in November, I get up to find the sun blasting through the clouds. Dad notices it too. The dining table is in the bay window in his bedroom. It's so huge it's almost like sitting in a shop window with a totally uninter-rupted view of the street. As he eats his porridge, I see him looking at the people passing outside – the lady up the road going for her newspaper, mums walking their children to school, our neighbour, a taxi driver, returning from his night shift.

'What's the weather like, love?' he asks.

'A fantastic day,' I say. 'Lovely bright blue sky.' As I spot the glint of enthusiasm in his eyes, I realize too late where this is leading. 'But it's very cold, Dad. Don't forget, it's autumn.'

Too late. Dad is not to be so easily deflected. As he hurries his breakfast, I fear what's in store. It's November. There's a chill wind. But Dad is taking a position of blissful ignorance of everything ninety-six years of life have taught him about weather conditions and he's champing at the bit to get outside.

I should be admiring his gung-ho attitude but actually I'm irritated. Suddenly, I've been catapulted back into a re-run of when the girls were little and wanted to go and play outside in the rain. I'd have to go into a long explanation of why it was a terrible idea. They'd get wet. They'd get cold. Sometimes, nagged and badgered, I'd give in against my better judgement. Finally, I'd get them stuffed into wellies and raincoats and out of the door. They'd play for ten min-utes and then reappear, miserable and bedraggled, stamping muddy wet footprints all over the kitchen floor. It would be exactly as I'd predicted. Infuriated with them and with myself, I would snarl: 'Well, maybe next time you'll listen to me.'

Now I want to snap at Dad. 'For heaven's sake, can't you see how daft this is?' But, even as the words flash up in my brain, I know I can't actually say them. It's not just that I don't have the heart to scotch his plan. After all, if he wants to go to all the effort of getting out into the garden and sitting in a deckchair in the biting cold, so be it. I point outside. 'Dad, it's sunny but it's really cold.'

Dad is unconvinced. The truth is that I'm battling hard to keep at bay the moment when it becomes my place to tell my dad what he can and can't do. We are teetering closer and closer to this every day as Dad's familiarity with the world outside fades. The more the ties loosen, the more he wants to push any decision-making my way. But, every time, I pull back – for both our sakes.

I'm determined to prod him into making decisions and choices, even ones that are as impractical and inconvenient as this one. What sensible person in their twenties, let alone in their nineties, would imagine sitting out in the garden on a chill November day? It's harebrained. But I'm not going to stop him, because making it possible will help him preserve his dignity and his confidence and keep him engaged. I know this isn't just about what's best for him, but what's best for me too. Dad's my dad. He's not my child and I'm damned if I'm going to treat him like one, however much I'm tempted to, however much he sometimes seems to want it. It's not my job to protect him from himself (not yet, at least). It's not my job to help educate him for the future. It's not my job to mother him. It's my job to help him be happy, as far as I can.

And so, here I am in my Driza-Bone coat, lugging out Dad's garden chair. Dad's watching impatiently from the window. Now here he comes, tottering across the terrace on his walking frame. I've helped him into his fleece-lined car coat – an ancient and much-loved item of clothing barely worn since Dad came to live with me. Dad sits in his chair and, as I disappear to the kitchen to make him a cup of tea, I wonder how long it will be before common sense wins the day against his mania for sunshine. As I breeze back ten minutes later, I can see Dad fighting hard to save face and pretend his fingers aren't freezing and his nose isn't dripping icicles. And I do something I never did with the girls – I pretend that this had been a great idea but now it's time to call it a day.

'Brrr. It's much colder than I expected,' I say. 'You must be freezing. Why don't I take your tea inside for you?'

Dad beams with happy relief. 'Well, it looked so inviting and it was nice to poke my nose outside, even for a few minutes,' he says as I help him up and we walk inside together. And the funny thing is that, although it was so short-lived, Dad's little venture into the garden actually was a good idea. He stays bucked up for the rest of the day. I don't know whether it's the simple pleasure of having walked outside or whether it's the satisfaction of having chosen to do something, however insignificant, and followed it through. But he was right.

Andy and I marvel once again at Dad. For this brief period Dad is the focus of our lives. Like indulgent parents, we talk endlessly about his quirks, his habits, the funny things he says and does. Caring for Dad, sharing a love for Dad, has brought Andy and me even closer. It's strange to know someone so well, to have known them from the very beginning of your life, and then to get to know them even better at the end of someone else's. And I feel quietly smug that I have made this happen. And also surprised that one simple decision should have led here.

But it is oddest of all to look back and think that, when my marriage ended, I expected that I would soon be living totally alone. These days I'm too busy, too preoccupied, and too happy to give Richard more than a fleeting thought. And when I do, it's with mixed feelings. I loved him very much and I can't help but regret things ended as they did. But how lucky am I that such unexpected happiness was around the corner? I haven't seen Richard since Dad moved in, but I hope that wherever he is and whatever he is doing, he is happy, too. Life – as I discover even more acutely from this precious time with Dad – is too short to fritter away being miserable.

FOURTEEN

HOME, AT LAST

We're undeniably a hotchpotch household. There's me and the girls – Elise has decided to take a gap year, so she's still here full-time. There's Dad and there's Andy and Milo. I can't believe that once the house seemed like a mausoleum. Now it's more like the National Gallery when there's a blockbuster on and you're standing on tiptoe just to see the pictures. Elise is in and out with her friends, and Frances and Sibylla are frequently around, often with little Nancy. Far from feeling burdened by the roles of mother, daughter and carer, I'm getting the greatest satisfaction from presiding over the jolly chaos in our home. What's really wonderful is being able to indulge Dad the way he indulged me.

Dad has a wooden box in his hankie drawer. He's kept spare cash in it for as long as I can remember. Now it's my job to keep it topped up.

'I only want a few bob to give the kids now and then,' he says. And that's true – Dad hasn't been in a shop or bought anything in almost two years. He always used to give the girls coins – £2 coins were a particular favourite. 'They're too heavy for me, you take them,' he would tease. I see just how much it pleases him to treat his grandchildren whenever Frances visits with Nancy.

'Have you got some money I can give that pretty little girl to buy chocolates?' he asks as they are about to leave.

Too late, I remember that the box is empty. And I have no spare cash. Dad will feel disappointed if he can't give Nancy something. I beckon Frances out of the room and explain the predicament. She rummages in her purse and produces a £10 note which I sneak into the box while Dad isn't looking. Dad calls for his box, beckons Nancy over and, with an indulgent smile, hands her the note.

'I know a little girl who likes chocolate,' he says.

Gamely, Frances thinks she ought to protest. 'But Grandpa, there's no need. Nancy has more money than I do,' she says.

'In that case, you'd better have it,' says Dad without missing a beat. And, as he smiles fondly, Frances pockets her own £10 note.

Dad has always been the most loving, caring grandpa. When Ellen was eight and Dad was eighty-five, my Aunt Mary visited from Canada. She brought Ellen a book: *My Grandfather and Me: A Memory Scrapbook for Kids*, which Ellen spent weeks painstakingly filling in.

I'd forgotten all about it. When I come across it one day, I show it to Dad. All the quirky little memories and funny spelling mistakes make us both laugh. She had written that her favourite sport was swimming. Dad's was skipping. She wanted to be 'wise and kind just like my grandfather', while Dad wanted to be 'young' just like her. When they're apart, lots of things remind her of her grandpa – especially the smell of Kit Kats. Dad kept a supply in his fridge, just for the girls.

We remembered how the girls' favourite time with Dad was their weekly Saturday-morning visit. While Richard and I did the weekly shop, the girls sat in Dad's kitchen while he cooked them a fried breakfast: the only time in the week they had such a treat. They loved this tradition so much that we carried it on long after they were old enough to be left alone in the house. About once a month for years and years, they also went to Dad's for a sleepover. It was always the same ritual. They'd watch an *Inspector Morse* video together. Grandpa would doze off, waking at 10 p.m. – just in time to shoo the girls off to bed with hot water bottles.

The only time Grandpa ever shouted at the girls was on one of these sleepovers. They must have been around nine and ten and were squabbling furiously in their bedroom. Hearing the hullabaloo, Dad came storming in to discover that, in all the mayhem, they'd pulled his bedroom curtain clean off the track. He was incandescent. But not about the curtain. He was afraid that they had hurt themselves.

Living with Grandpa is poignant – more so perhaps for Elise than for me. Seeing him every day, watching his body gradually slow down, it's impossible to pretend we haven't reached the very last act. He's been much more of a father to her than any other man in her life. He's loved her, championed her, protected her like no other male. He may be ninety-six but she is only eighteen – far too young to lose someone so important.

'I never want him to die and I know he's going to. And every day it gets more evident that's going to happen and that makes me sad,' she admits one day.

As she talks, I feel a cold grip on my heart. She's right. Dad has become such an integral part of all our lives in the last year, it's harder than ever to imagine our lives and our home without him. He's made us a family. How will we go on without him?

When Dad moved out of his flat, I was acutely aware that I was unpicking his home, making all the decisions you hope to leave until someone dies: which furniture to keep, which to give away, which of Mum's possessions – because, of course, her taste was stamped on everything – I could finally bear to say goodbye to. Mercifully, there wasn't a great deal. My parents liked good-quality furniture, but they hadn't cared much for knick-knacks.

When they were posted to Germany, they put all their possessions into storage. A few months later, there was a fire at the depot and everything was destroyed. The only things they really regretted losing were the family photos. If they'd been remotely acquisitive before then, they certainly weren't after that. There are very few possessions that have ever meant anything to Dad. All his memories are in his heart.

I felt lucky that I was doing all this while Dad was still with me. Now, when I drive past the flat where he lived, it's with a great sense of relief. Dad's safe with me. But now I see it is going to be immeasurably harder to unravel things once he dies. My home has become his, and his presence has seeped into every corner and cubby-hole.

Just how bittersweet for us all this last phase of Dad's life is hits home just before Christmas, when Dad's only surviving sister, Pat, comes to stay from Newcastle. She's ten years younger than him and bright as a button. Although Dad is thrilled to welcome her, his frailty is all too evident. He's seen her often in the last few years, but it takes him a long while to accept that this white-haired grandma of eighty-five with a charming Geordie accent is his little sister, when his memory of her was as a baby in a pram. How has she got so old? Where have all the years gone? At first, he's only really comfortable talking about the long distant past.

'You were the bane of my life,' he chuckles. 'I'd want to go off and play cricket with my pals and our mother would insist I took you too. So I'd wheel you off to the cricket pitch. And then, blow me, every time I was about to go into bat you'd start howling. I'd drop my bat, rush off to rock the pram and immediately get bowled out.'

During Pat's visit, details of his childhood seem to be spotlit. One evening, Pat reminisces about the time the family cat ended up trapped in their old-fashioned range oven. The children only discovered her when they lined up at bedtime to collect their pyjamas, which were kept in the oven during the day to warm.

'And there was that poor cat, gasping for breath.' Pat smiles. 'Do you remember, Jimmy, our father got her out and revived her with a drop of whisky on a teaspoon. He could be so harsh, but he did love animals. Now what was that blasted cat called. Do you remember?'

'Tibby,' said Dad without missing a beat. And it's as though he's been talking about the cat every day for the last ninety years.

I decided to take the opportunity of Aunty Pat's visit to throw a family party. Simon joined us from Edinburgh. My nieces turned up along with Nancy. We had a huge family lunch party in Dad's room. Cake crumbs were all over the floor, Milo scampered around the furniture pursued by Nancy, and, in the midst of the mayhem, sherry glass in one hand and wreathed in smiles, was my dad.

He was thrilled to see everyone, if a bit perplexed. He took me aside the first evening.

'Is there something I need to know, something you're not telling me?' he asked.

'Like what, Dad?'

'I just don't understand why everyone is here.'

'They've all come to see you.'

'Yes. But why now?'

'Well, as Aunty Pat is visiting, we thought it would be lovely to have a family get-together.'

Dad looks relieved. 'Thank the Lord for that. I thought for a moment that everyone was here to see me off.'

'As if!' I laughed.

But of course the truth is that his life is drawing to a close. He knows it and – although I try not to dwell on it – I do too. That's why everything about this unexpected time with him is so precious and so bittersweet. Sometimes I look back and wonder how I could have paused for even a nanosecond before offering Dad a home. He has given me so much more than I have ever given him. But then he always has. And one of the greatest gifts he has given me is hope.

All will be well.

POSTSCRIPT

Dad died peacefully in his sleep on 19 April 2013 after contracting pneumonia. He had just celebrated his ninety-eighth birthday. We had all hoped that he would reach a hundred, but, although he still enjoyed his tea and biscuits and made a big point of laughing at Laurel and Hardy dvds, it sometimes seemed he was doing it all just to please us.

In those last few weeks before he died, he talked increasingly about the past. At times it seemed as though long-dead loved ones were more vividly present to him than we were. He talked a lot about his mother, who died at barely half the age he was and before he even got married. When he woke in the night, he didn't call out for us any more but for his beloved elder sister, Kitty, who died in 1999. Sometimes I felt he really believed he was that little boy back at home in Newcastle, waiting for his life to begin.

Perhaps it was Dad's way of signalling he was ready to join all the people he fervently believed were waiting for him. And it's a great comfort to know how ready he was to say goodbye.

It would be selfish to feel sad for Dad because he died exactly as he would have wished – with nothing left undone or unsaid. And I know that I will always look back on these years with Dad as among the happiest in my life.

Every day a funny anecdote, one of Dad's quirky sayings or – best of all – a memory of his unstinting love for me, pops into my head. I'm incredibly grateful that I had this precious time with him. It was brief but so intense. Selfish or not, I just wish that it had lasted even longer.